Presented To:

____

By:

____

Date:

____

apples & chalkdust™

A Teacher's Journal

Vicki Caruana, America's Teacher

An *Apples & Chalkdust*™ Book

HONOR HB BOOKS

Inspiration and Motivation for the Seasons of Life

An Imprint of Cook Communications Ministries • Colorado Springs, CO

08 07 06 05 04 10 9 8 7 6 5 4 3

Apples and Chalkdust™: A Teacher's Journal
1-56292-279-3

Published by Honor Books,
An Imprint of Cook Communications Ministries
4050 Lee Vance View
Colorado Springs, CO 80918

Developed by Bordon Books
Designed by rmdtulsa.com
Produced by Grasshopper Productions

Printed in China.

Introduction

Every day in classrooms across the world, young faces look to their teachers for clear instruction and patient guidance. Teaching is a hard job, and teachers often need encouragement. But more than that, they need time to reflect and to think about whether they are meeting God's call upon their lives as teachers.

Apples and Chalkdust™: A Teacher's Devotional Journal offers encouragement from stories and reflections that will inspire you to write about your own aspirations and reflect on your teaching experiences each day. You will read about teachers such as yourself who are facing the challenges that teaching students presents and who are making decisions to renew, revise, and even to completely rebuild their methods and attitudes toward students and teaching. Read the entries in this book and respond to the prompts, and you will become more self-aware as a teacher and more able to become the kind of godly and innovative educator you always dreamed of becoming.

Vicki Caruana

What Does Your Garden Grow?

Each school has its own unique culture.

A small school will look and function differently from a large school. An inner-city school may look dramatically different from a rural or suburban school. Elementary is different from secondary; private is different from public.

Where the differences lie are not just in the structures themselves but in the values and beliefs of the inhabitants.

Look deep into a school, and you can see what is cherished. Walk the halls, and you will see what they value.

Walk into a school that looks sterile—white blank walls with no adornment and complete silence—and you will feel as if you have walked into a hospital. This school's leaders believe that students are there to be cured by their teaching.

Walk into another school with colorful walls covered with students' artwork—where teachers' doors are adorned with their personal style—and you will see a school that values students' creativity and teachers' personalities. It is a welcoming atmosphere, one that fosters growth.

Where do creative minds prefer to flower? They prefer a place where there is light, warmth, and plenty of food.

**IS YOUR SCHOOL A PLACE FOR GROWTH?
IT COULD BE, IF YOU CHOOSE TO BE A TILLER OF THE SOIL IN YOUR SCHOOL.**

Some of the ways I would like to make my classroom and school environments that encourage growth include . . .

"What is honored in a country will be cultivated there."
–Plato

Do It Your Way

Teaching eighth-grade science was Susan's passion. She effectively covered the subject content and inspired her students to ask questions. Most days she could be found at the center of huddled eighth graders who were trying to catch a glimpse of some scientific phenomenon.

Her principal, Mr. Dawson, was from "the old school." He saw disorder when students crowded around her. He saw unprofessional conduct in her enthusiasm. He didn't see what he expected to see: students working quietly and a teacher lecturing while using the overhead projector.

During a conference, the assistant principal warned Susan of his forthcoming negative evaluation. She muzzled her disbelief as she strained to maintain the appearance of professionalism.

Realizing that it was his perception that her students weren't learning, she knew she had to prove otherwise. Calmly, she explained her philosophy and invited him to return the next day to her class.

That day, she carefully orchestrated a lesson that showcased her students' grasp of a scientific method. They performed beautifully, as if on cue. Once Mr. Dawson was satisfied with her teaching technique, Susan was free to teach in her own way.

Fair or not, there will be times in teaching that you, too, will have to satisfy the doubts of others and prove yourself.

SOMETIMES YOU NEED TO GIVE OTHERS WHAT THEY WANT BEFORE YOU CAN DO WHAT YOU WANT.

Some ways I believe I can help others to better understand my style include . . .

"People only see what they are prepared to see."
–Ralph Waldo Emerson

Are You Willing?

"I don't have to listen to you!"

"What will you give me if I do this?"

Karen's head was swimming with the voices of her indignant students. It was the first week of school, and she had already lost her grip on her eighth graders. But then she wondered if she had ever had a hold on them in the first place.

Assignments had become bargaining sessions. If you do this, I'll do that. Finish this first, and then we'll do this. On and on it went, day after day. She wasn't teaching; she was begging! Karen remembered that when she was in school, she'd never have dared to argue with her teacher about the assignment. The teacher had the last word then. But not anymore.

Yet she noticed that these same students never seemed happy or content. There was no joy in learning. There was negotiation in its place. Karen had played this game before and lost. It was time for a different strategy.

"I've got a deal for you," she began. "You work, and you'll pass. You don't work, and you'll fail."

Simple yet satisfying.

BREAK THE WILL WITHOUT CRUSHING THE SPIRIT— THAT'S GREAT TEACHING.

As I think about the most enjoyable classes I have taken, what actions did my teachers take to effectively enlist my cooperation?

"To learn to give up his own will to that of his parents or teachers, as we must to the Greatest Teacher of all, will surely make him happy in this life and in the life to come."

–Fanny Jackson Coppin

Leo Buscaglia

Best-selling author Leo Buscaglia grew up in an Italian home. He actually learned English as a second language. Upon entering school, Leo was branded as mentally deficient and recommended for placement in a special class. He was "written off" by those who believed they knew better.

Miss Hunt taught this special class. She was a caring, warm person, and she paid little attention to the labels placed on her students. Miss Hunt modeled a love of learning to all in her class and saw Leo as rich in potential.

In Miss Hunt's class, Buscaglia blossomed. After several months, she insisted that he be retested. The results placed him into the regular classroom system.

Miss Hunt's door was always open to Buscaglia. She encouraged him and convinced him that wonderful things were in store for him.

Do you know a child who has been "written off" or "lost in the shuffle" by parents, teachers, or other students? Perhaps you are a teacher, like Miss Hunt, who will give him or her the benefit of the doubt.

A HEART OF COMPASSION AND BELIEF CAN BE THE VERY THING THAT CAUSES A STUDENT TO "MAKE IT."

Where do I need to apply compassion in my classroom this year? In what compassionate ways can I make a difference for these students?

"The heart benevolent and kind . . . most resembles God."

–Robert Burns

Little by Little

Cheri watched closely as the aide fed Michelle. It was always the same—first the positioning of Michelle in the chair and strapping her in, then the bib, then the introduction to the food placed in front of her. Janice, the aide, reminded Michelle at each mealtime what time of day it was, what she was eating, and what she would do with the fork or spoon. It was a painstakingly slow process, yet Janice was always full of encouragement and patience, something Cheri had been lacking lately.

Her intermediate varying exceptionality class may have been small in comparison to a regular fourth-grade classroom, but the demands were infinitely greater. Cheri had taught it for ten years, and she could feel burnout right around the corner. Many of her colleagues had already left this kind of classroom and were always amazed to hear that Cheri was still at it. They weren't the only ones who wondered why.

"I see so little progress," she said to her husband. "I think this will be my last year teaching this class."

Her principal was not happy with Cheri's news that she wanted to transfer. He knew how difficult it was to integrate a new teacher into this kind of situation.

On her last day, Cheri fed Michelle herself. As she lifted the spoon to her lips, she saw it! A smile! "Did you see that?" she asked.

"Yes," said Janice. "And it was all for you."

Cheri rescinded her resignation.

Sometimes just the simplest of steps forward are enough to encourage us to continue.

Have I dismissed small gifts of encouragement lately? Small things that have brought me encouragement lately are . . .

"People seldom see the halting and painful steps by which the most insignificant success is achieved."

–Annie Sullivan

Me? A Teacher?

Chad wondered what his friends would think. He knew that his new job not only would surprise them, but it would incite laughter! Chad, a teacher? No way! He had never really liked school himself, and he had struggled more than some. But after years in a job he didn't train for or like, he knew he needed to change. Becoming a teacher was not his first choice, but it wasn't that far-fetched either.

Chad's famed soccer career had come to a crashing end when he wrenched his knee. Yet now, following surgery, it was stronger than ever. His degree in science and a love for coaching was all he needed to convince himself that teaching in a high school might be a way to satisfy both loves. Midway through his teachers' training, he received a job offer from a prestigious high school.

"What are your goals for your students?" the principal asked during Chad's interview.

"I know this will sound idealistic, but I want them to love science. I want them, for maybe the first time, to see their connection to this place we call home. I want them to leave my class intent on making the world a better place to live." Chad paused. "And I want to be for them what every patient teacher was for me—hope."

Chad knew it sounded like a reelection speech, but he couldn't help it. He meant every word. For the first time, he felt he was right where he belonged.

THOSE WHO CAN, TEACH.
THOSE WHO WISH THEY COULD ONLY COMPLAIN.

The ideals I want to inspire my students to meet are . . .

"Education has for its object the formation of character. This is the aim of both parent and teacher."
–Herbert Spencer

Be Prepared

Lesson plans are just that—plans. They don't just appear! Yet there are times when all teachers feel as if they don't have time to write down strategic plans.

Do you know teachers who "fly by the seat of their pants"—who always seem to be rushing around to gather materials at the last minute and aren't quite sure what page they are on until the kids tell them?

Granted there are too many things teachers have to do that have nothing to do with teaching, and no one likes to take work home. A teacher's time is a precious commodity.

But the time spent in a classroom trying to decide, What are we going to do today? is not yours. It's your students' time.

Modeling time management and efficiency is an important part of the teaching process.

Your principal, fellow teachers, students, and your students' parents all watch how you manage your time. Your time management showcases your values and speaks of your priorities.

What are you spending your time on today? How much time are you investing in those things or people who matter to you most?

SHOW YOUR STUDENTS THAT THEY MATTER TO YOU.
GO TO CLASS PREPARED.

I know I make the best use of my time and my students' time when I . . .

"It takes time to save time."
–Joe Taylor

The Daily News

Glen surveyed the students in his senior journalism class. It had been a long and challenging year. So many of these students had been with him since their freshman year. He remembered their first days together as if it were yesterday. They could barely put complete sentences together, let alone independently run the school's newspaper. He thought that by the end of their senior year, they would be quite proficient in their skills. But for some reason Glen was still waiting—waiting for these seventeen- and eighteen-year-olds to show their full potential.

No one seemed to be able to concentrate on this last issue of the newspaper. Their minds were filled instead with signing their annuals, summer plans, and summer loves. Glen felt as if he were putting this issue together by himself. That's not what he had trained them to do. They had everything they needed to make it in the real world—or did they?

Two years later Glen ritualistically flipped through his morning paper. His eyes fell on the editorial page where a new columnist held the prized spot. He squinted his eyes to be sure he was seeing right. There in front of him was the byline of one of his former students. The title of his column was, "Those Who Give Us Wings." The carefully crafted story was about an old journalism teacher who had given this author his wings.

Be patient.
Even a butterfly can't fly until his wings dry.

The last time I discovered hidden potential in a student was when . . .

"There is nothing in a caterpillar that tells you it's going to be a butterfly."
–William H. Danforth

Yelling

Susan's high expectations for her students sometimes led to some frustrating moments. She taught seventh grade and found she was raising her voice frequently just to get the students' attention. Susan hated to yell. It wasn't in her nature, and it was extremely frustrating. Although it had some shock value, mostly it just gave her a sore throat.

Susan needed a better way to get her students' attention—something that would do the job without the stress. She had always thought she had good control of her class. Now she wasn't quite sure. There had to be a better way.

Later that week she attended a workshop with 200 other teachers. Many of the teachers hadn't seen each other in quite some time, and the initial visiting created quite a commotion.

The leader, impervious to the noise, announced in a normal voice, "If you can hear my voice, clap twice."

Then, as the clamor decreased, she said, "If you can hear my voice, clap three times." After a smattering of applause, the room grew quiet.

That simple demonstration of control was exactly what Susan was looking for. She couldn't wait to apply it to her own classes that very next week.

OPEN YOUR IMAGINATION TO NEW AND CREATIVE MEASURES TO CAPTURE THE ATTENTION OF YOUR CLASS. LEARN TO DIFFUSE FRUSTRATIONS BY PLACING YOUR ENERGIES INTO SEEKING POSITIVE, ACTIVE SOLUTIONS.

Some creative ways I can get the attention of my class are . . .

"An idea is salvation by imagination."
–Frank Lloyd Wright

The Play's the Thing

Serena's attempt to fill in for the drama club leader was falling apart. She'd had no previous drama training, and even though she'd agreed to do this out of loyalty to her friend, she was regretting her decision. The students were unruly at best. They came to club unprepared, not knowing their lines. Serena knew her authority was being challenged and she needed to do something about it quickly.

Two of the students who held the lead roles in the play were especially rude. In fact, they constantly harassed one student and brought her to tears on more than one occasion. Serena had warned them that if their behavior continued, she would pull them out of the play. She hoped her threat would never have to be carried out because opening night was in two weeks!

Again they showed up unprepared, and a tearful understudy fled the auditorium before rehearsal even began.

"You made the wrong choice," Serena scolded, and out they went.

Her drama coach friend called her that night furious that her best actors had been thrown out of the play. But Serena's decision stood, and she knew on opening night that it was the right one. The cast gave her a dozen roses presented by the formerly tearful understudy, who that night had the lead.

Make sure double standards never exist in your classroom. Wrong is wrong, no matter who commits it.

Have I allowed favoritism to color my decisions in the classroom? What steps can I take to rectify the situation and prevent it from happening again?

"Good discipline is a series of little victories in which a teacher, through small decencies, reaches a child's heart."
–Haim Ginott

Protective Parents

On first impression, Mrs. Gladstone was the parent most teachers dream of. She volunteered in the classroom two mornings a week, and she was a partner in her daughter's learning.

However, as the year progressed, Mrs. Gladstone's involvement became overwhelming. She started calling the teacher at home on the weekends. She was at her daughter's side for every field trip, whether she was needed or not. She began showing up for lunch every day.

While the teacher appreciated Mrs. Gladstone's intentions, she could tell that Natalie was uncomfortable with her mother's constant presence.

The teacher tried to dissuade Mrs. Gladstone from coming on field trips and encouraged her to cut down her lunch dates a bit. But Mrs. Gladstone nervously refused the advice. She wasn't ready to let go.

Rather than causing unnecessary tension, which could potentially damage the teacher-parent relationship, this teacher decided to change her strategy. She included Natalie in more group activities when her mother wasn't there. It took extra effort, but in the end it was a situation which benefited everyone.

In dealing with potential parental conflict, remember that some of the best results can be derived from compromise.

BE GRACIOUS AND UNDERSTANDING IN DEALING WITH PARENTS, KEEPING IN MIND THAT THEY ARE ENTRUSTING YOU WITH THEIR MOST TREASURED GIFTS—THEIR CHILDREN.

Some situations with parents that I need to pray about are . . .

"Don't find fault. Find a remedy."
–Henry Ford

Sight Unseen

Mandy eyed the roomful of fifth graders and desperately wished she were somewhere else, anywhere else! Then to add to her apprehension she caught sight of her reflection in the glass doors and cringed at her lack of hair, hollow eyes, and less-than-rosy complexion. The chemotherapy had done its job. The cancer was gone, but the calling card it had left was hard to ignore. What would the children think? She was afraid that all they would do is stare at her; they'd never hear the story she planned to tell.

The library was abuzz as the students watched Mandy walk onto their makeshift stage. She settled into the chair and unpacked her guitar. Mandy was sure she heard muffled giggles from the back of the room. She knew that it wouldn't be long until she had their attention, but for the wrong reasons.

After ten minutes of musical storytelling and quick changes, Mandy looked briefly into the eyes of a girl in the first row. Those eyes were laughing. But it wasn't her patchy hair or the dark circles under her eyes that made the girl smile. It was the escapades of Scooby-Doo that Mandy spun with her guitar. At the day's end, students surrounded her and asked questions. But they weren't the kinds of questions Mandy expected. "How do you make your guitar sound like a truck? What are those knobs for at the top of the guitar?" Relief flooded Mandy as she realized that they had seen her after all—the real Mandy, not the shell.

GOOD STORYTELLING IS A LOST ART. IT DISTRACTS THE MIND FROM WHAT IS SEEN AND DRAWS IT INTO WHAT CAN ONLY BE IMAGINED.

One way I can use storytelling in the classroom this week is . . .

"Good teaching is one-fourth preparation and three-fourths theater."
–Gail Godwin

An Olympic Moment

As chairman for the Special Olympics in her district, Laura Burns did everything she could to include as many students as possible in the games each year. The more competition there was, the better the athletes would be who would rise to the top. As a marathon runner herself, Laura knew the pleasure and satisfaction attached to competing in a challenging event. Then an unexpected honor presented itself to Laura and her district.

With more than a hundred students from her district competing in Special Olympics, carrying the torch from one point to another was especially challenging. She wondered how she could include all her students in this special honor. Because she was a runner, Laura was asked to do the actual running, while her students would watch. But to Laura, that wasn't good enough.

The day came, and everyone squinted as they watched the horizon for the runner who would pass the torch to Laura. "There he is!" someone shouted and a roar of cheers went up from the gathering crowd. Laura was ready for the handoff.

As the runner neared her position, Laura began running with her one hundred students ahead of her in a line. After the torch was passed successfully, Laura took a split second to sense the warmth of the flame and close her eyes in thanksgiving. Then she passed the torch on to the student closest to her, who ran ahead to the next runner.

YOU'VE PREPARED THEM WELL.
KNOW WHEN IT'S TIME TO PASS THE TORCH.

Some ways I can pass the torch of learning on to my students are . . .

"Those having torches will pass them on to others."
–Plato

With the Greatest of Ease

Fa•cil•i•ta•tor - n. One who makes things easy or less difficult.

Gwen stared at the image displayed by the overhead projector and wondered, *Am I a facilitator?* The workshop had seemed monotonous until this issue was introduced. And now Gwen was really wondering about herself. She taught advanced classes, and her students always seemed to be struggling.

She thought back over her teaching style. Overheads, lecture formats, note taking for students, use of textbooks and other resource materials—all of it was standard issue in teaching. But did it all "make things easy or less difficult" for her students? Gwen doubted it.

For some reason, she couldn't go back to business as usual at school. This workshop had really gotten under her skin. Finally, out of desperation and hoping for some peace of mind, she did what any good teacher would do. She looked the word up: Facilitate.

She learned that it means to accelerate, advance, enable, promote, and serve. It doesn't mean to complicate, discourage, hinder, or obstruct.

Gwen's shoulders slumped, and her head fell. She had wanted to challenge her students, but she realized at that moment that she hadn't been giving them the tools they needed to meet the challenge. That was the day Gwen became a facilitator.

ARE YOU A FACILITATOR?

What teachers did God provide in my own life who facilitated me? How can I further facilitate my own students' learning?

"The art of teaching is the art of assisting discovery."
–Mark Van Doren

The Main Thing

As a student teacher, Carl was thrilled with all of the fun and innovative things he had the opportunity to introduce to his students. Unbeknownst to him, his supervising teachers were taking care of the plethora of other duties, leaving him with a false perception of freedom as a teacher. Before he realized it, he had given in to the routine and lost touch of his sense of purpose.

As a new teacher, it isn't long before innovation is traded for familiarity. Many college graduates enter their first classroom, finding there is far more awaiting them than they could have ever imagined. They discover themselves under an avalanche of paperwork from students, the principal, and the district. Creativity and enthusiasm can easily be squelched by the overwhelming and unseen demands of the classroom.

Eventually Carl realized his dedication was waning. He knew that assigning and grading work wasn't teaching, so he refocused his attention and developed healthy boundaries for himself, his students, and the pressing daily requirements. As a result, the flashes of brilliance and creativity once again entered his classroom. His students flourished, and teaching became his rediscovered passion.

More than anything else, students need you to be a leader who is able to reinforce the fact that they are worth more than all the homework you could ever assign.

REMEMBER, THE MAIN THING IS TO KEEP THE MAIN THING THE MAIN THING.

What sparks your passion? What do you need to ask God to give you in order to keep that passion alive and bring the flame to the forefront of your day?

"The secret of success is constancy to purpose."
–Benjamin Disraeli

Judge Not

by Helen Peterson

Beth had just accepted a full-time teaching position at another school in the district, scheduled to start the following fall. Since her current assignment was a temporary one, she was grateful and excited for the chance to have her own class. She was going to miss the friendships of teachers, the principal, students, and parents at her present school, but she was ready to take on the responsibility and commitment to the new school.

Much to her dismay, when she announced her news in the teachers' lounge, some of the veteran teachers were not elated. Instead, they recounted the negative experiences they had when teaching at that school. They told her she wasn't going to like it there.

Beth listened quietly to their laments, but in her heart she decided she was going to love teaching at that school. She was going to find the teachers and principal interesting and supportive. She was going to appreciate the uniqueness of each student and teach them well. And you know what? She did!

Being happy and content is a state of mind. Look for the positive in every new change. Don't take the negative from others and assume it's all true. Bonding to a new environment is a challenge that needs to be met. Don't let others' opinions spoil it.

Search for the positive experiences in your journey, and you'll find them.

What are the positive experiences God has provided in my life as a teacher so far?

"The world is all gates, all opportunities, strings of tension waiting to be struck."
–Ralph Waldo Emerson

Open House

Tess inspected her room one final time before the parents arrived.

Students' work assignments were prominently displayed, and volunteer sign-up sheets were in plain view. The room looked organized and creative. This was Tess's tenth open house night, but she still got butterflies as parents took their seats at the children's desks. She felt that she was more on display than her students' creations.

This was her chance to make a good first impression. It might be one of the only times she would see these parents face-to-face. She wanted it to be a positive experience—one that instilled trust and confidence in her ability to teach their children.

The room was packed—standing room only. Tess circulated through the crowd, handing out papers listing items for a scavenger hunt. She thought that might break the ice. Within minutes children and parents were navigating the room looking for the places and things on her list. When at last everyone returned to their seats, Tess relaxed as she saw the smiling, excited faces.

It was a good start to a great year.

Putting forth the extra effort necessary to make parents feel confident about your teaching will produce enduring rewards. Each year, show yourself to the parents as capable.

Parents like to know that you are in charge!

I can increase parent confidence in me by . . .

"A true leader always keeps an element of surprise up his sleeve, which others cannot grasp but which keeps his public excited and breathless."

–Charles de Gaulle

The Testing

(Dedicated to the students in the education department at Clearwater Christian College)

The first time is always the hardest. It's always the most consuming and it's always the most sweet. Teaching future teachers was the most rewarding work Vikki had ever done. It had a definite domino effect, reaching far into the future. She laughed aloud as she remembered her own reaction to this teaching assignment. Assessment! How could she possibly make such a dry topic come alive?

Twenty-five college juniors and seniors in the education department of a small private college had gathered with a collective groan. This was a dreaded class—one avoided until the very end, when students had run out of all other options. All they knew was that it was boring but necessary and definitely hard. Vikki remembered when she had taken this same class. It was indeed all they feared. But she didn't want to see fear in their faces each week. She wanted to see intrigue and delight.

She brought them out of their comfort zones of reading, listening to lectures, and taking quizzes and expected of them professional standards, insights, and discussion. She modeled for them what she expected, and they rose to the occasion. The workload was heavy; but the support was strong, and victory was won! Students left her class equipped and motivated. Vikki collapsed with sweet exhaustion when the semester was complete. Now she watched as each of her students' lives touched hundreds more.

WHEN YOU HAVE A CHANCE TO TEACH TEACHERS, GIVE THEM WHAT YOU EXPECT THEM TO PASS ON TO THEIR STUDENTS.

If I had the opportunity to teach teachers, I would like to instill in them . . .

"We loved the doctrine for the teacher's sake."
–Daniel Defoe

George Washington Carver

Whenever George Washington Carver tried to attend a school, he was either quickly turned away or ridiculed because he was black.

Following the Civil War, it wasn't easy for former slaves to carve out a life for themselves. Even so, George pressed on.

The Listons were a white couple whom George befriended while at Simpson College in Iowa where he was the only black student. They owned a bookstore, and he spent most of his free time there. Later George chose to attend Iowa State, and once again he was the only black student. Immediately, he was the object of racial insults. In a letter to the Listons, Carver complained about the way he was being treated.

Mrs. Liston took the train to Iowa State and walked the entire campus leaning on his arm. "The next day everything was different," Carver later explained. "The ice was broken, and from then on, things went very much easier."

Students who don't quite fit in for one reason or another sometimes just need a helping hand—not necessarily to help them reach but to help them connect.

IS THERE A STUDENT IN YOUR MIDST WHO COULD USE YOUR ENDORSEMENT TODAY? BE AN ADVOCATE FOR SOMEONE WHO REALLY NEEDS IT.

Is there anyone I know who needs an advocate? How can I lighten their load?

"A good deed is never lost; he who sows courtesy reaps friendship, and he who plants kindness gathers love."
–St. Basil

The Sound of Music

The Sound of Music was Perry's favorite musical from childhood. As a music teacher, he reveled in its simplicity and grace. He loved music and loved children, so his career choice was an easy one. But what of those children who had neither the talent nor the desire to immerse themselves in the magical world of music? The Von Trapp family singers are a legacy to many. But is it because of their devotion to music or their devotion to one another? Perry knew.

Perry made it a point to meet with teachers from every grade level over the summer. What were they learning that he could put to music and therefore make it easier for all of them to learn? "After all, we all learned our ABC's that way," Perry explained during one such meeting. By the time school started, he had written songs to teach the states and their capitals, the continents and the oceans, the presidents, the prepositions, and even the categories of animals.

The point of his effort was not to produce a concert of his original songs. It was not to attract publicity to his ever-vulnerable music program. It wasn't even to entice students to take up a musical instrument. The end result Perry hoped for, and ultimately found, was that there would be joy in the journey—that the music would move the minds and the hearts of his students.

USE YOUR OWN PASSION
TO IGNITE THE PASSION INSIDE YOUR STUDENTS.

How can I give my students joy in the journey this year? What do I need to ask God for so that my own journey can be joyful?

"What will a child learn sooner than a song?"
–Alexander Pope

The Right Path

Patricia's mother was a teacher. Her grandmother was a teacher. Both of her sisters were teachers. Yet her mother encouraged her to do something else. She said, "You can do better."

To appease her mother, Patricia became a speech pathologist. She graduated with honors and went to work in a notable hospital for children.

After three years with different clients every hour and an environment in which she was uncomfortable, she found herself dreading the start of each new day.

The symptoms of dissatisfaction surfaced. Patricia began to be chronically late. She withdrew socially at the hospital. She was tired all the time and began to hate the career path she had chosen.

One day, one of her young clients was about to be dismissed from her care. The parents asked Patricia if she would accompany them to a meeting at the new school and explain their son's speech difficulties to the speech teacher.

Patricia went willingly. She had always been curious about the school setting. After their meeting, she wandered throughout the school soaking up its atmosphere and thinking, *This is where I belong!*

The very next day, Patricia took immediate steps toward changing her path and moving into the school system. For the first time in her life, she was content and fulfilled in her work. She had accomplished her own dream . . . she had followed her own heart.

CHOOSE YOUR OWN PATH, AND STICK TO IT.

Is there another path in my life that better fulfills the way God designed me to be? What is the next step to getting there?

"If you don't like the road you're walking, start paving another one."

–Dolly Parton

Reproof

Bob simply couldn't get comfortable in his school environment. There were so many things he wished were different. To add to this he was the only male teacher on his team.

If there were more men here, he thought, *maybe I'd feel more a part of things.* He had been a math major in college and went into teaching as an afterthought. It was not his original intention, and he was uncertain in his teaching role.

Constantly he analyzed situations looking for things that could have been done differently. And his colleagues tired of his constant deliberating on these matters.

Most of the time, the other teachers just quietly ate their lunch as Bob complained. One day Bob muttered, "If only things were different. . . ."

Finally, one of his friends spoke up and said, "But they aren't different. Get over it, and go on!"

Bob looked stunned, just as if he had been slapped across the face. After a moment, his face softened, and he realized his friend was right. It was that very statement that enabled Bob to transform his perspective, move on, and enjoy his position as a teacher.

Hearing the truth can be painful, but try to remember that a friend's reproof is rooted in love and can be an opportunity for change.

THINGS CAN BE DIFFERENT ONLY IF YOU MAKE THEM DIFFERENT.

What truth do I need to accept that will enable me to let go of roadblocks to my own happiness? What do I need to ask God for that will help me move forward in my life?

"It is a sheer waste of time to imagine what I would do if things were different. They are not different."
–Dr. Frank Crane

A Seat of Honor

Sally Hill loved her job. Admittedly, teaching in a one-room schoolhouse in a black community had a myriad of challenges. It wasn't just the matter of teaching multiple grade levels or the inconveniences of such cramped surroundings that weighed on Sally's mind. It was the frustration of not being able to give her students all they would need to make it in this cruel world. And little Rosa, as smart as she was, lived with ridicule day in and day out.

Sally knew that showing favoritism toward students was not recommended, but if she could shelter and protect Rosa if only for those hours during the school day, she would feel as if she had accomplished something. One day the other kids teased Rosa mercilessly, and she began to cry. Sally motioned for Rosa to come up to her desk. From then on, she let Rosa sit up front with her whenever she felt sad.

Rosa Parks knew it was special to sit up front. And years later, when she insisted on sitting up front on a bus in Montgomery, Alabama, she knew that it was wrong that somehow she wasn't considered special enough to sit there.

SOMETIMES SPECIAL TREATMENT IS
THE KINDEST ACT OF ALL.

Some things I can do to make a student feel special are . . . Some things I need to ask God to do to help me feel special are . . .

"One person can make a difference, and every person should try."
–John F. Kennedy

Learn from Mistakes

Natalie's previous principals had trained her to be a good teacher—one who accepted responsibility willingly and expertly.

Her move to the district office was one she welcomed and believed was the next step for her. Although she missed the classroom, she felt she'd be able to make a difference in her new position.

Her first assignment as a resource teacher was to track down a missing camcorder reported stolen from a local high school. Natalie felt confident in her new position and, since the school's assistant principal was a former colleague, she felt quite comfortable approaching him with this situation.

Unfortunately, as she began to question the assistant principal's handling of the robbery, her confidence was perceived as intimidation. She not only met with resistance, but she also alienated the one person who could have given her answers.

Realizing her mistake she tried to apologize, but instead of seeming genuine, she came across as unprofessional. A complaint was filed, and Natalie was demoted to desk work the very next day.

Natalie jumped rashly into a role she thought had inherent power and respect. The truth is that power and respect are earned, not bestowed by virtue of the position.

When you are in a new situation, give yourself some time to learn the ropes; and your decision making will be much more effective.

TAKE THE TIME TO LEARN THE CULTURE OF YOUR NEW ENVIRONMENT BEFORE YOU ACT.

An important aspect of my school environment that a newcomer can't see right away is . . .

"When you make a mistake, admit it; learn from it and don't repeat it."
–Bear Bryant

Honor Guard

Dan Shea paced up and down the aisles of his tenth-grade English class. It was the last day of their standardized testing. Dan was tired, and he could tell his students were as well. One in particular could barely hold his head up. Dan knew that this behavior would probably result in a low score on the test. This was one of his best students and he cringed at the thought of the repercussions of a poor score on this test.

During their break, Dan consulted with his colleague next door. His advice was not what Dan had expected.

"Dan, you know the consequences if students do poorly on this test!"

"I know. I hate to think which class he'll be placed in next year," Dan said.

"No! It's not the kid I'm worried about. It's you!"

"Me?" Dan was confused.

"His failure is a blemish on your record. Do whatever it takes to prevent that, if you know what I mean."

Dan walked back to his room in shock. *Was he suggesting what I think he's suggesting?* he wondered. Dan sorted the response forms from the test booklets. When he came upon his sleepy student's form, he paused. He scribbled a note and attached it to the front of the form. The best he could do was inform the administration that the student was sleepy. Dan realized then that teachers are tempted to cheat for the same reasons students are.

Honor above all!

I feel pressure against my integrity in these areas:

"Don't care what others think of what you do; but care very much about what you think of what you do."
–St. Frances DeSales

Spice It Up!

Are you in a teaching rut? How do you know?

Can you teach that algebra lesson in your sleep? Be careful—you might be teaching while your students sleep!

Strive to be a "seasoned" teacher—one who doesn't lack vigor. A seasoned teacher is one who brings variety, zip, and delight into the classroom.

Something that is seasoned wakes up the taste buds and tempts the recipient to want more. Once tasted, it is craved!

Do your students get excited by your teaching? Do they want more?

How can you become seasoned instead of growing stale? What can you add to your repertoire that is unusual and interesting? How can you be surprising and tantalizing? You don't have to be a sideshow. You just need to bring your teaching back to life.

All around you are opportunities to do things differently. Send away for that catalog. Enroll in that class. Go listen to that speaker. Find your own personal zest!

Not only will your students be coming back for more, but you will enjoy your own teaching again.

Spice up your teaching.
Bring a new excitement into your classroom.

Three ways I can immediately spice up my teaching are . . .

"You've got to continue to grow or you're just like last night's cornbread–stale and dry."
–Loretta Lynn

The Tutor

Angie Becker soothingly stroked her expanding belly as she watched Jonathon struggle through the algebra problem on the board. She had committed to work with him after school each day for this marking period. It seemed like the only way to give him the extra attention and time he needed to bring up his failing grade. Angie's pregnancy may have tired her physically, but she never tired of the satisfaction and utter joy she felt when Jonathon finally grasped a concept.

Teaching one-on-one in a tutorial way brings two people closer together. Angie felt both pride and affection for this student. He had become close to her as well. But one day, five weeks into their time together, Angie doubled over in pain. In what felt like a frenzy of activity, Angie was whisked away from school in an ambulance. The last thing she saw was Jonathon's concerned face as he stood helplessly at his desk.

Three weeks later, after the end of the marking period and a less than effective substitute, Angie returned to school. She eyed the pile of work to be graded, and her heart fell as she realized it was too late for Jonathon. As she sifted through that pile, she came upon a plain white envelope. Inside was a card, and on it was scribbled in Jonathon's less than perfect handwriting, "I'm sorry you lost your daughter. But please know you did real well with a son. I got a B! Thank you."

TAKE THE TIME TO MAKE SOMEONE ELSE'S DAY A LITTLE EASIER.

What can you do to make a difference in the life of one of your students?

"The man [or woman] who can make hard things easy is the educator."

–Ralph Waldo Emerson

The Team

Upon becoming an administrator, Madelyn felt overwhelmed. Although she had trained for this position and had obtained all the necessary degrees, she knew there was more to it than that. She had to depend on the counsel of those who were already there.

The trick was figuring out on whom she could depend. After a few months of getting to know her staff, she knew it was not really "her" staff. They were still quite attached to her predecessor.

This arrangement could have hindered the overall progress of the department. Madelyn couldn't be the expert in everything. Curriculum was her strength, but scheduling was not. Parent interaction was something she reveled in, but a public image was not. She needed people who could fill in the gaps and make the team whole. Though at times uneasy, she had to depend on the strengths of her team.

As opportunities arose, either out of resignations or transfers, Madelyn's mission was to scout out experts.

By the end of the second year, she felt that she finally had a dynamic team of players in her department and found it easy to defer to their judgment. It became evident that leading where she was strong was expected and preferred by all those involved.

EVEN IF YOU CAN'T HANDPICK YOUR STAFF, RELY ON THE BEST OF THEIR INNATE ABILITIES. WHEN THEY SHINE, THE TEAM SHINES.

Strengths that I offer a team would be . . .
Weaknesses of mine for which I would need to rely on others' strengths would be . . .

"I make progress by having people around me who are smarter than I am—and listening to them."
—Harry J. Kaiser

Homecoming

Christin cried as she walked out of her school for the last time. Yes, she'd miss the kids. Yes, she'd miss her friends. She'd even miss her mailbox! She knew the tears weren't logical, but they fell nevertheless. Her decision to stay home with her own children was applauded by some and criticized by others. And now as she walked to her car, all she could think about was what she was walking away from. Had she made the right decision?

As the beginning of the next school year rolled around, Christin felt disconnected and disoriented. She had always started school in the fall since before she was five years old. It didn't feel right to be at home. She began to daydream about what it would be like if she did go back to teaching. This life felt lonely. It was an unhappy first year at home.

Three years later, the beginning of the school year came and went without Christin even realizing it. She was so busy teaching preschoolers in her own home with her children that she didn't miss the school bell. Sitting with five four-year-olds on her living room floor was joyous.

At the end of one day, one of the moms from her little preschool paused at the door. "Christin, without your dedication, I don't think Jason would be ready for kindergarten next year. I just wanted to say thank-you."

IF HOME IS WHERE YOUR HEART IS, GO THERE AND FIND OUT WHAT WORK THERE IS FOR YOU TO DO.

Where is my heart leading me, and how can I achieve my call to teach in that place?

"The more you love what you are doing, the more successful it will be for you."
–Jerry Gillies

Conferences

Conducting a parent-teacher conference wasn't covered in Sarah's education courses. Once a teacher, she found that she was expected to meet with each parent at least once a year.

Most of her students were doing exceptionally well, with good grades and good behavior. But there were a few who were frustrating. She was dreading their conferences.

She started with easier conferences first, secretly hoping that the parents of the more difficult students wouldn't even show up.

After two or three conferences, Sarah noticed that once she conveyed the positive things about her students, parents responded with, "Please don't hesitate to let us know if Johnny ever strays." And Sarah wondered if the same might happen with the parents she was avoiding.

She called each of the parents of her most challenging students and told them at least one positive thing about their child. It wasn't easy, but it did force her to concentrate on the strengths of these students.

A few weeks later she scheduled their conferences. She repeated the positives and then enlisted help with the negative. She was encouraged to discover that these parents were just as willing to help and assured her that they would be supportive.

REMAINING POSITIVE OPENS THE DOOR FOR PARENTS TO WORK WITH YOU TOWARD SOLUTIONS.
TELL PARENTS THE POSITIVE FIRST.
IT MAKES THE NEGATIVE MORE PALATABLE LATER.

List a positive character trait for each of your students. Ask God to show you how to emphasize the positive and eliminate the negative.

"No act of kindness, no matter how small, is ever wasted."
–Aesop

The Power of One

Being a Mom, Wyn knew that her attitude and emotional state determined what kind of day she'd have with her family. If she was off, they were all off. What a terrible responsibility it is to be a human barometer. Even with this knowledge, it took Wyn a lot longer to recognize how she affected her students as well.

There were days when, for one reason or another, she just didn't want to be at school. There were days when she never stopped complaining. There were days that she couldn't smile, no matter how she tried. And on those days, her students' behavior mirrored her own. She believed their behavior was out of her control.

One day Wyn was notified that she had received the grant she had worked on all year. It would supplement her classroom in a variety of ways. But most of all, it was an accomplishment that reenergized her attitude toward teaching.

In the weeks that followed, she approached her job with a renewed sense of purpose and joy. Her students seemed to join in her enthusiasm, and they, too, had a renewed sense of purpose. The funny thing is that Wyn had had the power to change her students' behavior all along. But the first step had been to change her own.

WONDERING WHY YOUR CLASS SEEMS A LITTLE HO-HUM? TRY BRIGHTENING YOUR OUTLOOK, AND SEE IF IT IS REFLECTED IN THAT OF YOUR STUDENTS.

How's my perspective and attitude? I feel energized when . . .

"Nothing great was ever achieved without enthusiasm."
–Ralph Waldo Emerson

Walk in Line

When Flora walked her class down the hallway toward the lunchroom each day, she was determined to teach them how to walk straight, tall, and with purpose in mind. She didn't want them wandering aimlessly down the corridor.

Flora expected her kindergartners to learn the right way to do things, and learning how to walk together in line was their first opportunity to do so.

When older students would walk down the hall opposite her class and were rowdy and misdirected, she would point it out to her students. "See that class? Let's show them the right way to walk respectfully." Her students would proudly stand at attention, passing the older class with quiet sophistication.

New students to her class would be indoctrinated in line-walking their very first day. Flora would say, "Let me show you how it's done." And then she would walk forward, leading her class like a mother duck leading her focused ducklings. Her students caught on quickly. It was truly a thing of grace and beauty.

Teachers are leaders. Lead your students on the right path by showing them what you want and how you want it done. Leading your students in the way that they should go begins with the simplest of tasks.

Let them see how you walk.

THE WAY YOU TRAVEL THROUGH LIFE IS THE MOST POWERFUL LEGACY YOU CAN GIVE TO YOUR STUDENTS.

The legacy I want to leave to my students is . . .

"If you want to be a leader with a large following, just obey the speed limit on a winding two-lane road."

–Charles Farr

Fallen Angel

Cindy listened intently, surprised to hear that her friend had left her job as a school social worker to work in a hospital setting. "But, Kendra, you seemed so happy at your first school. You told me you loved the people in the community and felt that you were making a real difference in their lives. What went wrong?"

Cindy had been Kendra's closest friend in college, and she had shared Kendra's goal of becoming a school social worker. Confiding in her made Kendra feel better about her choice.

"After my first school closed," began Kendra, "I had to take a job in a much larger district. I had to divide my time among five schools and wasn't able to form relationships with the students as before. My whole job description changed. It seemed that I was unofficially in charge of doing all the things no one else wanted to do. If a parent wouldn't sign certain placement papers, it was up to me to confront them. If a student was physically disruptive in class, it was my job to contact the authorities.

"I started losing the love I once felt toward people. I felt myself becoming cynical and distrusting and began to forget why I'd become a social worker in the first place. I miss working with students, but my new job at the hospital is fulfilling; and I'm starting to feel needed and loved again."

Cindy was happy that Kendra had found a place where she could use her talents, but she was saddened by the thought that the school system had lost such a caring person who could have been an integral part of helping students get a good education.

SOMETIMES IT'S THE UNSPOKEN EXPECTATIONS THAT DRIVE GOOD PEOPLE AWAY. GIVE EVERYONE AROUND YOU THE SUPPORT THEY DESPERATELY NEED.

I really feel supported when others . . .

"You can work miracles by having faith in others. To get the best out of people, choose to think and believe the best about them."

–Bob Moawad

First Aide

Joan Steffand's new job as a teacher's aide would be a welcome change. The school was within walking distance of her home, and she would be working with a teacher who was well-respected. Days after being offered the job, she was in the classroom unpacking supplies from the summer. She had one concern. The last aide who held this job had been with this teacher for fifteen years. How could this teacher come to depend on Joan as much as she had depended on her last aide? Joan knew nothing of how this job worked.

"Hi. I'm Stacy Welch. And you must be the answer to my prayer!" Stacy Welch immediately picked up a pair of scissors and joined Joan to cut out bulletin board decorations.

"Joan Steffand. Happy to be here." Joan eyed Stacy warily. Was she really as at ease as she appeared?

Stacy could see that her new aide needed encouragement. "Joan, I'm so grateful you were available. The thought of beginning this school year alone was not a happy one."

"But you've taught this class for fifteen years. You don't really need an aide," Joan said.

"It's not a matter of ability, Joan. It's a matter of preference."

"But I'm only an aide," said Joan.

"This is our room, these are our students, and this is our job. Together we can make a difference." Stacy's resolve swept away any apprehension Joan had.

Including others in your success is a vital part of creating an atmosphere of teamwork and cooperation in your classroom.

The last time I felt included and appreciated was . . .

"Every great pitcher needs a great catcher."
–Casey Stengel

Compliment

by Ailene Doherty

Dr. McGuire was the principal at Lackspoor High School. He was undoubtedly the most efficient person the teachers had ever worked with. He was, however, one of the most frustrating administrators on the staff. He never complimented them, neither did he criticize. He just issued bulletins stating what should happen and when.

After Alicia had been in the system for many years, she learned that Dr. McGuire's wife was very ill. She knew a sentimental card would not be appropriate to send to him. So she decided to bake her culinary specialty, an angel food cake, and give it to him. If he didn't approve of such a gesture, she couldn't be too severely punished, for she already had tenure!

Alicia's delight was unbounded the next day when Dr. McGuire handed her a ragged piece of a brown paper bag on which he had written a note that read, "You are not only a good cook, but a very good teacher."

Alicia went to her classroom, clutching her first compliment from her principal, marveling at the power of that small act of kindness.

The power of a genuine compliment is never wasted and is the best investment you can make in those around you.

INVEST IN YOUR STUDENTS,
SHOW YOUR BELIEF IN THEM, COMPLIMENT THEM,
AND ACKNOWLEDGE THEIR GIFTS.

A compliment that really influenced me to excel was . . .

"I can live for two months on a good compliment."
–Mark Twain

Under Construction

The announcement was met briefly with applause from the teachers, but only moments later it turned into regret and concern. They all knew that the construction of the addition and remodeling of the existing buildings was well overdue, but the thought of teaching amidst the coming chaos was not inviting. Principal Lanning and his teachers were bracing themselves for a difficult two years.

The cafeteria was the first to be relocated, and students had to eat in their classrooms. The teachers' workroom was next, and the copy machines and supplies were scattered throughout the remaining untouched areas. Tensions rose, and parents complained that it was an unsuitable learning environment. Absenteeism on the part of teachers and students rose.

Lanning, who still had five years left, seriously considered early retirement. But some teachers beat him to it, and those who remained looked to him for encouragement and leadership.

By the end of the first year of construction, parents had picked up the slack and the morale in the school slowly improved. When the weather was good, they had picnic lunches outside, and Lanning reinstituted recess. And once a month the PTA dipped into their budget and provided a lavish catered lunch for the teachers. By the end of the construction, they were all happy to have survived it, but they were also closer because of it.

A POSITIVE ATTITUDE IS SOMETIMES THE ONLY CHOICE YOU HAVE.

I can make a positive difference to my students if I . . .

"You gain strength, courage, and confidence by every experience in which you really stop to look fear in the face. You must do the thing which you think you cannot do."

–Eleanor Roosevelt

What's Your Passion?

"Who was your favorite teacher, Diane?" Julie asked her friend as they watched their children play together on the beach.

"That's easy. Mr. Danker, my tenth grade Biology teacher. He was strange, that was for sure. But I still remember everything we did in his class. He was also into taxidermy, and above each of our desks hung some sort of stuffed animal!" Diane excitedly explained.

"Oh, how gross!" Julie was horrified.

"No, it was cool. Each week we had a test, and it was difficult. But we could improve that grade if we dared. We could gain extra credit if we ate, without gagging, something he brought in—like oysters, squid, or even pig's feet!" Diane was quite animated now.

"I remember that we created a huge animal collage all through the year. You could only put something on it if you could identify it and tell one defining characteristic. At the end of the year, part of our final exam was to find a particular animal on that collage, identify it, and remember that characteristic. You know, I haven't thought about that in years. Why don't our children's teachers teach like that?" Diane's joy ended abruptly.

Are we teaching like that? Can your students see your passion in what you teach? If you don't have passion, find it! Only then can you light that same flame in your students.

How can I show more passion for what I teach to my students?

"A dull teacher, with no enthusiasm in his own subject, commits the unpardonable sin."

–R. C. Wallace

Holiday Ho-Hum

Patricia's head was swimming with all the information she had acquired from both her diversity and sensitivity training. As a beginning teacher she was especially aware of doing a good job and meeting the needs of all her students, no matter how impossible it seemed. Yet all she could think about that day was how she would celebrate the coming holidays in her classroom.

Her own memories of holidays in school were special, and as a first-grade teacher she couldn't imagine just ignoring them as her principal had suggested. She stared at the blank bulletin board for what seemed like hours, unable to make up her mind. She didn't want to dictate any one holiday to her students.

"Well, I'm going to decorate it with things that make me feel good," she said and began cutting out construction paper decorations.

"What are you making?" an early arrival asked. But before Patricia could answer, the six-year-old began drawing decorations of her own.

Before the bell even rang, she was on the floor with ten children making holiday decorations for their bulletin board—each slightly different, each just as excited to make this bulletin board their bulletin board.

So Patricia didn't have to figure it out after all. The children had ideas of their own!

INVOLVE STUDENTS IN THE PLANNING. IT'S ONE OF THE GREATEST MOTIVATORS.

A bulletin board filled with things that make me feel good would have to contain . . .

"When one door of happiness closes, another opens; but often we look so long at the closed door that we do not see the one which has opened for us."
–Helen Keller

Inclusion

Jan waited patiently as her department head worked his way through the team-meeting agenda. It was the second time she had been scheduled to speak, but she had the sinking feeling they wouldn't get to her this time either.

Jan's learning-disabled students were struggling in the regular classroom environment—not because of their ability, but because there was a definite feeling of exclusion.

Jan needed to address this issue as an advocate for her students. After all, who else would speak up for them. Jan was willing to do whatever it took to change the way the needs of her students were perceived, but unless the team gave her a chance to talk, she wouldn't be able to make that needed difference.

Finally, it was her turn. Jan stuck to the facts, but not without emotion. Revealing her compassionate heart, Jan demonstrated to the other teachers what it was like to sit in a class where students were ignored, everything sounded garbled, and much of it looked like nonsense.

As she made her final statement and returned to her seat, her team looked at her as if they had seen her for the first time. They were finally able to understand the helplessness her students felt.

Never allow an opportunity to pass where you might be able to be an advocate for your students.

REMEMBER THAT YOU SPEAK FOR YOUR STUDENTS. AND ALSO REMEMBER THAT SILENCE CAN BE SEEN AS AGREEMENT.

Ways I feel God calling me to speak for my students are . . .

"Don't limit a child to your own learning, for he was born in another time."
–Rabbinical saying

Teacher Appreciation

The teachers' lounge began to fill with the aroma of various delectables. Sharon Mazer placed the bouquets of fresh flowers on each table. There were crisp, white linens, good china, polished silver, and even crystal goblets at each place setting. Classical music was piped in through the intercom system. Everything was perfect. Even the fluorescent lighting couldn't ruin the mood of this Teacher Appreciation Day.

Sharon and her makeshift crew of parents led the teachers to tables and began to serve them this lovingly prepared brunch. The teachers were overwhelmed by their kindness. Some even cried. Sharon couldn't wait until the end of the brunch. She had something special planned.

As the brunch wound to a close, Sharon spoke eloquently about how teachers had touched her life as well as the lives of her children. "There is no greater calling," she said at the end. Then, as if on cue, her servers approached each table with what seemed to be a bill in their hands. The teachers opened them with hesitance.

Oohing and ahhing exploded from the tables. The PTA had given each teacher a gift certificate to their favorite teacher supply store. The teachers were grateful, but Sharon only wished she could give them more. After all, how could she really repay people who had sacrificed so much just to teach.

EVEN IF YOU'VE EXPERIENCED ONLY SMALL DOSES OF APPRECIATION, KNOW THAT THE WORLD COULDN'T PROGRESS WITHOUT YOU.

The last time I really felt appreciated occurred when . . .

"Your children need your presence more than your presents."
—Jean Kerr

Easy to Please

With only three years left until he could retire, Mr. Latham longed for a peaceful, problem-free year. He was in a school he had led for eight years. This was his last stop. He wanted to leave it on a successful note.

Since his elementary school had more than 800 students, the district built a new school to house the ever-increasing south district student population.

This welcome relief turned into a nightmare as angry parents petitioned rezoning committees. Latham was flooded with special attendance permits daily, but this was just the beginning of his frustrations.

Long-awaited construction at his school had finally begun. However, it displaced many classes and lasted much longer than ever projected.

Teachers were frustrated and parents were even more frustrated. The kids seemed fine. The adults were having all the problems.

Long meetings and lengthy correspondence occupied much of his time. His attempts to please the multitudes were met with skepticism and distrust. At the end of the year, Latham knew it hadn't been his best. He began to wonder if this should be his last year. He thought more about it and decided that next year would be a better time to retire. He decided to lead the situations instead of letting the situations lead him.

Upon what gauge are you basing your goals and decisions? Follow your goals, not the path which follows frustration.

In what situations am I focused on pleasing too many people? I feel God showing me that the best path for me to follow in this case is . . .

"I cannot give you the formula for success, but I can give you the formula for failure—try to please everybody."
—Herbert Bayard Swope

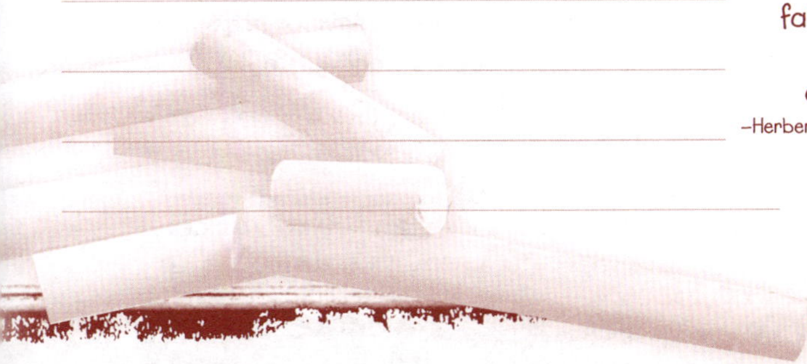

Arbor Day

Ms. Samuels' sixth-grade earth-science classes were involved in an extensive study of how plants affect their environment. An arborist, a horticulturist, and an environmentalist all came to speak to them about how shrubs and trees might have an impact on their local surroundings. Upon inspection of the school grounds, it was discovered that many of the trees were well over one hundred years old. As exciting as that was, it became quickly apparent that most of the trees were sick.

The dying trees posed several health and safety problems for the school. Huge infestations of insects lived in them; large limbs were threatening to fall; and root systems were the culprits of uneven sidewalks. Ms. Samuels was proud of their discovery and presented their concerns to the local school board. Unfortunately, the school board didn't see the problem in the same desperate light as the others did.

I really thought this exercise would teach the students how they could make their world a better place, Samuels thought. *All it did was teach them that it wasn't worth trying.*

The next week Ms. Samuels was called into the principal's office. The principal pointed to the morning newspaper and asked, "Was this your doing?" The article featured ten of her students and listed their concerns for safety at the school due to the dying trees.

She smiled to herself, realizing that they had learned a way to make a difference after all.

A lesson in real-life problem solving carries students into a promising future.

What can I introduce to my students this year which will make the world a better place?

"If you plan for a decade, plant a tree. If you plan for a century, teach the children."
–Anonymous

Light a Fire

With the new standardized test of basic skills in place, teachers scrambled to stay on top of their curricula so their students would perform well on the test. The demands were great, and the time was quite limited. They found themselves teaching around the test—not the preferred way to teach, but it seemed to be a necessary evil.

Ken, a math teacher, was worried about a group of students who were falling behind. He had only six more weeks to complete the study of multiplication, yet some students were still struggling with the beginning concepts. What could he do?

The time needed to go back and reteach these few students just wasn't there. But neither was Ken willing to accept the idea that some students must fall through the cracks.

He realized, just as King Solomon did centuries ago, that knowledge for knowledge's sake is meaningless. He decided to focus his attention on inspiring his students with a passion for learning. This inspiration would reach far beyond any one test; it would prepare them for the test of life.

With this goal in mind, he made the best use of the time he had. By adding enthusiasm, props, and visuals to his teaching during those last few weeks, he inspired a combustible hunger for knowledge within his students.

It's the fire you light under your students that matters. It filters through the cracks and reaches students at every level.

THE FIRE FOR LEARNING THAT YOU LIGHT IN YOUR STUDENTS WILL AFFECT THEM FOR A LIFETIME.

I influence best when my own fire is lit. I keep that fire burning best when I . . .

"Education is not the filling of a pail, but the lighting of a fire."
—William Butler Yeats

50/50

"He's not pulling his weight around here!" Latisha finally complained aloud. She was tired of covering for Jim, tired of filling in the holes he left in their students' learning. This team-teaching thing just wasn't working out. Math scores were considerably lower for all their students. Something had to be done, and Latisha was done doing it herself.

Sitting in her principal's office, Latisha listened as Mr. Balton tried to encourage her.

"I've known about Jim's weaknesses for quite some time," he confessed. "That's why I paired the two of you. I thought he'd learn from you since you are such a good teacher."

Latisha didn't know whether to be angry or thankful. He'd known all this time that Jim was weak in math?

"But I was wrong," he continued. "First, forgive me for expecting you to do my job for me. It's up to me to make sure my teachers are getting the help they need. Second, don't give up on us; we'll work this out together."

"Well, I'm willing to do my part if you're willing to do yours. But what about Jim's part?" Latisha said.

"How about this idea? You give 100 percent and I'll give 100 percent. Part of my responsibility is to mentor Jim. If we both give 100 percent, the students win!" Balton watched Latisha for signs of agreement.

After a long pause, Latisha finally smiled. "Yes, our students deserve all of me, not just part."

TEACHING IS LIKE A MARRIAGE. IT'S 100/100, NOT 50/50. GIVE IT YOUR ALL, REGARDLESS OF WHAT ANYONE ELSE DOES.

When I am tempted to give less than my all, I am encouraged to think about . . .

"Every job is a self-portrait of the person who does it. Autograph your work with excellence."

–Erik Erikson

Teachers Are Students

As teachers, we are perpetual students. Yes, we may take another college course here or there to renew our certificates, but we also learn from our own teaching experiences.

Through the act of teaching, we learn how to resolve conflicts effectively. We discover how to talk so others will listen. We remember what it's like to be a student, so we tread with care.

Remember the first time you had to teach fractions and it wasn't until the end of the lesson that you finally grasped it yourself? That's not something to worry about; that's something to celebrate!

Experiencing the learning process along with your students provides you with wonderful insight.

Your students will know they've really learned something when they can teach it to someone else. Give them opportunities within the classroom to teach or mentor others.

To educate is to be a part of a cycle of learning and teaching.

When you attend an eye-opening workshop, teach others what you have learned. When you make a mistake, encourage others not to do the same.

Have a humble heart when it comes to this business of teaching. You never know what you might learn or from whom you might learn it.

DON'T BE AFRAID TO BECOME A STUDENT OF YOUR STUDENTS.

The last great thing I learned from my students was . . .

"By learning you will teach; by teaching you will learn."
–Latin proverb

Tell Me Why

(Written especially for the education students at Keuka College, New York)

Amy was anxious to discover the tricks of her trade. What works? What doesn't? Which method, approach, or strategy would help make her first year of teaching successful? Amy knew that when learning something new, she should ask someone with experience. So when a well-respected teacher visited her campus, she did just that.

"Why?" the teacher replied.

"What do you mean 'why'? Please tell me what makes a successful teacher," Amy pressed.

"It's not the who, what, where, or even how questions that will get you your answer. Start by asking 'why.'

"As children, the question 'why' is most common and natural, yet we squash it. It makes grown-ups uncomfortable. 'Why' makes a person think—sometimes about things they don't want to think about. Yet in order to improve, in order to reach the unreachable, we must begin by asking 'why.'

"Why does Jane learn quickly, yet John does not?

"Why isn't this math curriculum working?

"So the most important question isn't how I do what I do," the teacher continued. "The most important question is 'why' I do what I do."

WRITE IT DOWN, MULL IT OVER,
BUT FACE IT TODAY AND EVERY DAY.
EACH DAY ASK YOURSELF "WHY," AND THEN YOU'LL
FIND OUT EXACTLY WHAT YOU NEED TO DO.

Some areas in which God is leading me to ask "why" more often are . . .

"Teaching is not just a job. It is a human service, and it must be thought of as a mission."
–Dr. Ralph Tyler

Environment

Laura is a teacher who is very self-confident and, to be honest, has a good right to be. She has a knack for accurately assessing situations. Unfortunately, her timing isn't always right, and she often runs into resistance.

This year when Laura started at a new school, she was excited and very much at ease even though it had been five years since she'd stepped foot into a classroom. Her enthusiasm and creativity caused her to take on new activities and programs.

Laura was used to spearheading new ideas, but she wasn't used to a principal who was resistant to that kind of energy. She was stopped at every turn. Any new idea was quickly shot down. Her principal was comfortable with the status quo—no more and no less.

Laura's innovation had been squelched and her bitterness grew. Frustrated, she decided that this school was not where she belonged, and she impulsively put in for a transfer for the next year.

Even though it is a principal's job to get to know the teachers, it is just as crucial for a new teacher to take time to get to know the culture of the school. What is valued? What are the rules? Who has the power?

Being watchful, learning, and working within the parameters of your school's environment helps ensure your ability to make changes and adjustments later, when it really counts.

LEARN YOUR SCHOOL'S CULTURE; ADAPT AND BECOME PART OF THE MOLD BEFORE YOU TRY TO BREAK IT.

My school's culture is distinguished by the characteristics of . . .

> "All communities have a culture. It is the climate of their civilization."
> –Walter Lippmann

Lend An Ear

Tori couldn't believe it. She felt just as she had in high school. She had been serious about school, but many of the girls around her hadn't. All they did was chatter, especially while the teacher was talking. They commented on so-and-so's outfit or hairstyle. They made fun of those who weren't as popular or as pretty as they were. Tori had become annoyed at these girls who got in the way of her actually learning something. And now, during her first faculty meeting, she was experiencing the same frustration.

Several other teachers who were sitting right behind her were talking in loud whispers. Tori strained to block out their voices so she could hear her principal. But the distraction was too great, and Tori found herself eavesdropping on their conversation. Believe it or not, they were critiquing the attire of each faculty member. Then they giggled at the bow tie the seventh-grade science teacher wore. Memories of more high school horrors!

When the meeting ended, Tori nonchalantly turned to get a glimpse of the gossipers. They were picture-perfect, dressed in the latest styles, with perfectly manicured nails and flawless skin. Tori slipped out of the auditorium, praying that she would be unnoticed, and hid in her classroom.

You've got to be kidding! she thought. *No wonder some teachers don't get treated like professionals; they're acting like they're still in high school!*

LISTEN TO YOURSELF WHEN YOU TALK. YOU MIGHT BE SURPRISED AT WHAT YOU HEAR.

If someone listened to me talk with my colleagues they would hear . . .

"Stop talking so much. You never see a heavy thinker with his mouth open."
–George Washington Carver

Give It Time

by Ailene Doherty

Amy was an enthusiastic and optimistic first-grade teacher. By Thanksgiving her students were progressing even faster than she had hoped—all except for Jonathan.

Jonathan seemed so withdrawn. Amy wondered what she could do to make the classroom a happier experience for him. Maybe she could move his seat near children who would encourage him. Maybe she could offer him some sort of reward or assign him a mentor.

Then she was hit by a thought. Maybe she was trying too hard to change Jonathan. Perhaps he simply needed time and patience. Amy relaxed and decided to give him room to progress at his own pace.

Only a few weeks later, Jonathan went to Amy during recess and handed her a book, "This is my favorite book. Would you like to read some of it to the class?"

An amazing improvement. His first step. Ever so slowly the changes took place, and by the end of the year Jonathan was voted as the student who had made the most progress!

There will always be students who take longer to adjust and fit in. Sometimes all they really need is time, patience, and to know you are available if needed.

It takes some children longer than others to rise to the occasion.

Remember to give them time and not rush to fix a problem that may adjust itself.

Students who need more time and my prayers are . . .

"Little by little does the trick."
—Abraham Lincoln

Margin of Error

Group projects were always tiresome to orchestrate, let alone grade. Someone always ended up doing most of the work. Someone always became disgruntled. And someone always slid by doing nothing. Tensions rose and patience wore thin as students tried desperately to work together, something to which they were unaccustomed.

Barb had formed the groups herself this time. They were quite diverse groups, each member with a unique talent or strength. Each group had its own topic to study and present to the class. Today was presentation day. Barb had worked hard to comprise the groups of individuals who would promote efficiency and quality. It was her decision that was also on the line today.

One person in each group was designated as the speaker, the person who would present an overview of the project. Group One's speaker rattled off a five-minute overview of their project. When he was done, his group was speechless. The speaker had introduced the wrong topic. He was humiliated, and Barb was furious. How could he have made such a mistake? Barb had made sure each student knew his particular job in the group. They had worked for weeks on their parts.

Upon investigation, Barb realized that the mistake had been her own. She had taught them well how to do their parts. But she had neglected to show them how those parts work together.

THE NEXT TIME A STUDENT MAKES A MISTAKE, MAKE SURE THAT IT'S NOT YOUR MISTAKE YOU'RE SEEING REFLECTED INSTEAD.

The parts of past student mistakes that I need to honestly confess come from my neglect of . . .

"An error means a child needs help, not a reprimand or ridicule for doing something wrong."
–Marva Collins

Listen and Learn

Mary eagerly looked into the faces of her first class, fully expecting they'd look at her just as eagerly in return. However, eye contact wasn't easy to come by, and the only eagerness she saw was when they looked at the clock.

How do you compete with a clock? she thought.

Replacing a teacher in the middle of the school year was difficult enough. But taking the place of a teacher who had been overly harsh made the situation even more complex.

Mary wondered if she would ever get past the wall that seemed to exist between her and the students. Their level of frustration, though unspoken, was immense. Her search for wisdom had taken her only to textbooks and research studies, but she did not find answers there.

One night, as she was unable to silence her thoughts in order to sleep, she made a decision. She needed to stop trying to change her students and, instead, start trying to understand them.

She began to encourage her students in what seemed at times to be the smallest achievements, and she invested much more time in listening to them. By building up her students in their gifts and hearing them out on things, she created an amazing bond with them.

Even with her inexperience, she was able to find a connection with her students by simply showing them how much she really cared.

TAKE THE EXTRA TIME TO GET TO KNOW YOUR STUDENTS AND SHOW THEM THAT YOU CARE.

When I know I have connected with a student, I feel . . .

"If a child lives with praise, he learns to appreciate."
–Dorothy Nolte

Pass or Fail?

Stan had taught social studies at Melham Middle School for fifteen years and had the reputation of making history come alive for his students. They always seemed to thrive and do very well.

But each year he discovered more and more students were lacking basic reading skills, hindering essential comprehension.

How did they get this far? he wondered.

Two days before final grades were due Stan had a conference with the principal. It seemed that two boys were failing not only his class, but every other class they were taking. The principal asked if Stan could see his way clear to pass them.

This seemed stronger than a request; it seemed to be an expectation.

"I can't do that," Stan said. "They didn't pass. They didn't come to class. In fact, they did nothing!"

His principal still pressed. "They are too old. We need to pass them."

"Then someone else will have to do it," rebutted Stan. "It's not fair to them or to the other students who worked so hard."

Although another teacher decided to give the boys a passing grade, Stan knew that he had done the right thing.

You may someday have to be the teacher who cares enough about the future of your students to keep them at the same level until they really learn.

THERE WILL BE TIMES WHEN YOU MUST STAND ON PRINCIPLE, EVEN WHEN IT IS UNPOPULAR.

I feel God calling me to stand on the principle that . . .

"Be sure you put your feet in the right place, then stand firm."
—Abraham Lincoln

Einstein

Young Einstein was never considered to be a brilliant child. Intellectually, he even seemed backward. He didn't learn to talk at an early age. Little or none of his future ability was detected in early childhood.

By age ten, he was considered to be precocious, but in attitude only.

Even in high school, he was thought to be only average at physics and mathematics. It wasn't until Hermann Minkowski mentored him that his genius was recognized.

After that, things began to change for Einstein. His independence and self-confidence grew so much that it was difficult for any university in the 1890s to satisfy him.

His spark of genius became fully ignited when he got a job in the patent office. Suddenly he saw the physical insights interwoven with the heavy machinery in the patent shop. It was there that Einstein's mathematical genius took flight—and history took one of its biggest leaps.

How often does genius fall through the cracks of the school system? Our challenge as teachers is to find creative ways to nurture independent thinkers and creative souls, encouraging them to reach beyond their imaginations.

Is there someone in your class today who could be, like Einstein, a diamond in the rough?

PROVIDE THE GIFTS OF UNDERSTANDING AND ENCOURAGEMENT. YOU NEVER KNOW WHAT GIFTS YOU'LL ALLOW TO EMERGE!

One of the students in my class who reminds me of someone whose gifts haven't yet emerged is . . .

"Creative minds always have been known to survive any kind of bad training."
–Anna Freud

Prepare Ye

"How do you really prepare for your first teaching job?" Kal wondered aloud. He finally landed his first job with no time to spare. There were only two more days until pre-service. This was not how he had imagined it to be. He thought he'd be able to spend all summer gathering resources, working his way through the textbook, and lining up field trips and experts to visit his class. Instead, he barely had time to set up his grade book and number those textbooks.

Kal had the sinking feeling he would spend all year playing catch-up. And that's exactly what happened. He stayed barely one chapter ahead of his students. There was no time for him to plan field trips or devise any high-interest activities. So he fell into the habit of assigning the chapters, collecting homework, and giving tests. This was not the kind of teacher Kal wanted to be.

For weeks he skipped lunch to stay ahead of the paper pile. One afternoon a colleague stopped by to ask if Kal's class would be interested in joining his class on a field trip.

"It's last minute, I know. But Mr. Angler's class had to cancel, and I need to fill the bus. It would really help me out if you'd come."

Kal's despair turned to relief as he realized the gift this teacher was offering him—a chance to break out of the box he had backed into.

Share your creativity and resources with others. You may be their answer to prayer.

God is calling me to share the following resources and strengths:

"There is no shame in asking for help."
–William Glasser, M.D.

Balance

"Never smile before Christmas!" Most teachers know that there are some things you just don't do! And boundaries are a must when it comes to maintaining respect and order.

Common sense told Susan that it would be easier to ease up on her discipline at a later time than to attempt to become more strict. Yet, try as she might, she was unable to stick to that unwritten rule.

She loved children and wanted her kindergartners to have a sense of security.

She wanted them to feel safe and to know that they could make mistakes without fear of humiliation.

She remembered well the embarrassment of having to stand with her nose to the chalkboard for an hour in junior high because she didn't know the answer to a math problem.

She did not want to produce that same feeling in her students.

Susan believed, as so many teachers do, that part of teaching is to nurture. Students need to be encouraged to take risks and to grow in a learning environment where they feel safe. She understood that the love of learning is cultivated through encouragement, not fear.

As the year went on, Susan successfully maintained a structured but creative classroom.

Keeping a good balance in your classroom can be a challenge. Let your students get to know you as someone who is fun and fair—but never as someone to fear.

RULE WITH MERCY AND GRACE, AND YOUR REWARD WILL BE GREAT.

One way that I want to lead with mercy and grace is . . .

"Encouragement is oxygen to the soul."
–George M. Adams

Guess Who's Coming to Dinner?

Brenda watched the documentary about Japan with increasing interest as the reporters attempted to explain why Japanese students scored so much higher than American students on standardized tests. Three things jumped out at Brenda as being possible explanations. They had a longer school day and year. Teachers were highly paid and respected. Parents took major responsibility for their children's education and were very involved in their lives. Unfortunately, all these things were rarely found in the United States, if at all. "We are doomed!" Brenda said aloud.

One side note to the documentary captured Brenda's attention. It seems that teachers in Japan are required to visit the home of each of their students at least twice a month. Parents know that the teachers are there to check up on them as well as the children. Brenda realized that this was one idea she could incorporate. *Parents and teachers always seem to meet on school turf,* she thought. *Why not meet on the family's turf?*

After some calculating, Brenda figured she could visit three students per week. Her principal was impressed with her plan; it was the parents she needed to convince. After all, they were not used to a teacher making a social call. But how else could she really build a partnership with parents? The challenge was worth pursuing.

WORK SIDE BY SIDE WITH PARENTS. DO WHATEVER IT TAKES TO BUILD THAT BRIDGE.

I sense that God is calling me to work with my students' parents to . . .

"A problem is a chance for you to do your best."
—Duke Ellington

Frank Lloyd Wright

Frank Lloyd Wright's success as an architect was a direct result of the influence from his first teacher—his mother.

Like many of his contemporaries in the 1870s, Wright was schooled at home along with his siblings. His mother was always searching for opportunities to advance and improve the education of her children.

In 1876, the Wrights, taking advantage of the special railway excursion rates, traveled from Boston to Philadelphia to attend the Centennial Exposition.

At the Exposition, Mrs. Wright came upon a life-affirming discovery for her son, Frank. The new Froebelian "Kindergarten" idea was on display, and Mrs. Wright eagerly drank in the new concepts and applied them to her children's education.

Although Frank was past kindergarten age, the Froebel ideas were quite formative for him, and he attributed much of his architectural success to his mother's wisdom and vision for his life.

As a teacher, never discount the incredible influence a mother has on her child's education. Allow her vision to reinforce your efforts in the classroom.

Strong parental involvement is key to the success of a child's education!

BE GRATEFUL FOR PARENTS WHO INVOLVE THEMSELVES IN THEIR CHILD'S LIFE IN SUCH A WAY. THEY CAN MAKE YOUR JOB SO MUCH EASIER.

A way I can encourage parents to influence their child's learning is . . .

"One mother teaches more than a hundred teachers."

–Jewish proverb

Creature Feature

Carol Dome's classroom was noisy, crowded, and sometimes even smelled! But it wasn't her students' fault—it was the animals. Carol believed that elementary school is a time for exploration and discovery. Creation was up close and personal for her students, and they used any spare moment to observe and comment on their surroundings. The circle of life included them, and Carol's teaching helped connect them all. All except her principal, Mr. Dawsey.

All he saw upon entering her class was chaos. He didn't even know where to begin to conduct her teacher evaluation. He knew the students loved this teacher; he just wasn't convinced much learning was going on. Until one day . . .

The children were unusually reticent and calm when Principal Dawsey entered that day. One of the baby chicks, newly hatched, had died suddenly. Carol Dome was sitting in their midst on the floor, her hands cupped around the now still chick. Each child quietly opened their journals and wrote their reactions to this event. Then one child moved to the bulletin board and adjusted the growth chart of their animal nursery. Finally, another child fetched their book on hatching chicks and read aloud the section about problems during hatching.

Mr. Dawsey saw these children apply a myriad of skills that day, even in the midst of tragedy. Carol Dome's evaluation was a much clearer task to him now. Learning was indeed occurring—even for him.

THERE IS MORE THAN ONE RIGHT WAY TO TEACH.

How would you evaluate the learning going on in your classroom? What can you do to create an environment that helps your students apply what they have learned?

"Who dares to teach must never cease to learn."
–John Cotton Dana

Assignment Alma Mater

Eileen lingered at the locker, letting her fingers brush over the well-worn metallic numbers. Idly, she turned the combination lock and almost expected it to open. Of course it didn't—it hadn't been her locker in more than ten years! Looking down the all-too-familiar hallway, Eileen Dansk wondered if teaching at her old high school was such a good idea after all.

The first week of school brought with it even more nostalgic memories. Her homeroom buzzed about her presence and the fact that she still looked young enough to be in high school. It was then that she realized this wasn't a dream, but a reality that could easily overcome her. None of her students were in their seats, nor did it look as if they intended to sit down. Eileen stared at the pile of papers she was supposed to get these students to fill out. Her own experience in high school had not been all that pleasant. She'd never felt like she really belonged.

Her ninth graders didn't know that though, and Eileen capitalized on their ignorance. "I have thirty minutes to get you to fill out these forms. If you can do it in fifteen, then maybe I'll have time to tell you what it's going to take for you to really fit in at this school."

It's interesting how the promise of social acceptance motivates kids to pay attention.

YOUR OWN EXPERIENCES IN SCHOOL CAN BE USED TO IMPROVE THOSE OF YOUR STUDENTS.

Personal school experiences I can use to help my own students are . . .

"Calming down a noisy, rebellious group of adolescents is a lot like defusing a bomb. Careful, premeditated, calm responses are crucial to success."
–James Nehring

Picket Line

Vicki was well prepared for her new teaching assignment. However, it's never easy to start midyear. Squeezing through the adolescent crowd, Vicki approached her room. She was abruptly stopped by a picket line!

"No new teacher!" the signs glared.

Twenty-five sixth-grade gifted students paced in front of her classroom, unhappy that they had been assigned to a new teacher. Without hesitation, Vicki slipped between the protesters, pushed the call button to the office, and reported the disturbance. Gathering her materials from the desk, she began to write assignments on the board.

Just then her principal stepped in to let Vicki know that her students were on their way.

A deep breath accompanied by a quick prayer was all she had time for.

As the now subdued crowd reluctantly entered the room, Vicki welcomed them with a spirited "Good morning!"

Their defiant gazes barely met hers.

"We've got a lot of work to do, so let's get started."

Passing out some neon-colored paper she said, "I'd like to work with you on creative problem solving. First we need a problem. Any ideas?"

Reluctant hands went up, and so began the process of building a new class.

Sometimes the only defense for skepticism and doubt you will have is your own self-assurance and poise. But there's no better way to restore trust.

TRY TO TURN EVERY SITUATION, POSITIVE OR NEGATIVE, INTO A LEARNING EXPERIENCE.

What am I struggling with now that seems negative? I can make it positive if I . . .

"The ultimate measure of a man is not where he stands in moments of comfort and convenience, but where he stands at times of challenge and controversy."
–Martin Luther King Jr.

Stand at Attention

When Vanessa enrolled her five-year-old daughter, Kaitlin, in kindergarten she chose a private school. This school had a three-year waiting list, and Vanessa had put Kaitlin on it when she was two. She was excited to finally be able to meet the teachers and tour the facility with the eyes of a kindergarten parent.

The rows of desks could not have been more perfectly aligned. Each prospective child's name was displayed on his or her future desk. The bulletin boards were color coordinated, and the discipline plan was in plain sight in the front of the room. Each child had a construction paper bear with his or her name on it. Vanessa read the plan in horror.

Talking out of turn = take bear away

Moving out of seat = take bear away

Dropping pencil = take bear away

No homework = take bear away

Tardiness = take bear away

On and on it went. Vanessa's blood drained from her face as she asked, "But how do they get their bear back?"

The teacher looked at her in disgust. "Not until the next day when it starts all over again." This is the teacher Kaitlin would have in kindergarten? Vanessa politely thanked the teacher for her time and sprinted to the office to take Kaitlin off this hit list!

IN DISCIPLINE, BREAK THE WILL BUT PRESERVE THE SPIRIT OF A CHILD.

I try to preserve the spirit of my students by . . .

"Let early education be a sort of amusement; you will then be better able to discover the child's natural bent."
–Plato

First Class

Sandra had spent all weekend arranging and rearranging her classroom.

She decorated it with posters professing profound sayings. She set the desks in such a way that her students would receive the greatest impact from her teaching.

Finally, she sat on her stool at the front of the room and surveyed the setting.

It was perfect.

It had to be.

It was her first classroom.

Captivated by her thoughts, she imagined the events of the day to come. The student roster printed in her lesson-plan book would come to life as the twenty-five sixth graders entered the room. The students—her students—would eye her warily as she moved to the front. She knew her carefully written name on the board would stump them. That was all right. She hoped its perplexing spelling would break the ice.

This was a moment she would remember all her life—a moment she had waited for and dreamed of since she was a little girl.

Sandra refocused on the still empty desks. With a heart full of hope, she prayed that this year would be filled with many significant and memorable moments for both her and her students.

WHAT ARE YOUR HOPES AND PRAYERS?ON DAYS WHEN YOU WONDER WHY YOU EVER BECAME A TEACHER, CLOSE YOUR EYES AND RECAPTURE THE MOMENT THAT INSPIRED YOU LONG AGO.

I felt God calling me to pursue teaching when . . .

"Change your thoughts and you change your world."

—Norman Vincent Peale

Satisfaction Guaranteed?

Janice sighed heavily as she hung up the phone. Mrs. Baxter, the mother of a student with special needs, wanted a conference—again.

It seemed that she couldn't please this mother. Although their meetings always ended on a positive note, Janice was beginning to wonder what she could do to avoid them altogether.

This year had definitely been one with unusual challenges in Janice's classroom, and to be truthful, Mrs. Baxter usually had valid concerns.

This conference began just as all the rest—Mrs. Baxter restating her son's needs; Janice restating her desire to meet his needs. But this time Mrs. Baxter had a new question ready. "What level of satisfaction should a parent expect from your class?"

What a loaded question! Janice was speechless. Mrs. Baxter continued, "We both know that 100 percent is not realistic. Nothing and no one is perfect."

Mrs. Baxter went on to explain that after some soul-searching she knew that her own unusually high expectations had created some of the frustrations she was feeling over her son's school year.

Mrs. Baxter's humility struck a chord with Janice. She turned the question around. What were her expectations of parents? Were they realistic? Janice knew she had some soul-searching of her own to do.

A willingness to put forth the effort to understand each other opened the door for a wonderful relationship between Janice and Mrs. Baxter.

MAKE UNDERSTANDING YOUR PRIORITY BEFORE TRYING TO BE UNDERSTOOD.

I need to make understanding my priority in the following situations:

"People need to see how much agreement is possible between seemingly intractable opponents."
–Robert Redford

Did He Pass?

Rob looked at his list of students to be tested and cringed—twenty-four kids to test in three days! Rob's testing was only the first step in a very long process to qualify for placement in the school's gifted program. Only about 25 percent of those tested would actually qualify. And many of those tested were referred by their own parents. Dealing with the disappointment and sometimes downright indignation of parents was the least favorite part of Rob's job.

Rob could usually tell within the first few minutes of testing whether or not a child would pass his screening test. It was obvious that this second grader wasn't going to make the cut. After testing he met with the parent privately and relayed the results. He could sense her frustration. Rob thought, *Another parent who is absolutely convinced that her child is gifted.*

"Please, there must be some mistake," she said.

Rob responded with his all-too-familiar speech about how this test was not a full IQ test; it was only a screening instrument and her son could take it again next year.

"You don't understand," the Mom continued. "Mrs. Wickstrom is the best teacher here. She's our last chance to motivate Jon."

It's funny how some parents flock to one program or another. It's not always because they are an elitist or because the program is the popular place to be. Sometimes it's because a teacher has made it clear to all that kids are important.

A program is only as successful as its teacher.

The way I want to make it clear that my students are all important is . . .

"Start a program for gifted children, and every parent demands that his child be enrolled."
–Thomas Bailey

The Ah-Ha Effect

Not covered in any college textbook is the sensation of "Ah-ha!" when a student finally understands what was once an incomprehensible concept to him. Judy learned that firsthand when she tutored a boy diagnosed with a math disability. It wasn't her student's discovery that changed her, however; it was her own.

She had learned how to break the learning of a new concept back down to the concrete level if a student was having trouble. So when it came to fractions, a trip to the pizza parlor seemed in order. Not just because it would be fun, but because Judy herself had always struggled with fractions. Teaching the lesson step-by-step (including consuming the prop) led Judy to an amazing discovery—she finally understood fractions! For the first time in her life, she really understood them! This made teaching them not only easier, but more exciting.

Should it have taken Judy until she was twenty to fully grasp fractions? Unknown. What is known to her now, however, is the power of the Ah-ha effect. She knows that it doesn't really matter how long it takes, as long as it happens. Maybe a student just needs more time. What are you willing to do to ensure your students' success? Your work is not done until you hear, "Oh, I get it!"

Do you know which students "get it" and which don't? You should. Take the time and give more when needed.

Reflect on a time when you clearly saw a student grasp a difficult concept.

"My heart is singing for joy this morning. A miracle has happened! The light of understanding has shone upon my little pupil's mind, and behold, all things are changed."

–Anne Sullivan

TK (Teacher's Kid)

Elizabeth wondered how long she should wait. The school year was half over already. She watched as one of the fifth graders just barely got by. Being in the gifted program brought with it certain expectations, and this student wasn't meeting any of them. Elizabeth knew that in these cases she was supposed to request a reevaluation of the student to see if she still belonged in the program. But Elizabeth was hesitant. This child's mom was also a teacher of the gifted in their district and was well-respected. She knew she could be starting a war if she proceeded. Still, she sent the notice for reevaluation home.

Two days later, Mom, daughter, and the school's assistant principal showed up in her classroom for a meeting. Elizabeth was alone with her conviction. According to the assistant principal and the child's mother, Elizabeth's actions were unwarranted and unprofessional. Although Elizabeth's request for reevaluation was denied, she was glad that she had taken the risk of addressing the situation. Because of the meeting, Elizabeth discovered that the student had some health issues that were contributing to her lackluster performance in the classroom. The student's mom realized during their meeting that she should have shared that necessary piece of information with Elizabeth sooner.

While confronting this parent was anything but easy, Elizabeth felt good knowing that she had opened the lines of communication and would now be able to help this student succeed.

HAVING TROUBLE WITH A TEACHER'S KID (TK)?
REMEMBER TO HANDLE IT WITH GRACE.

Ways I would like to have other teachers handle my children are . . .

"The only reason I always try to meet and know the parents better is because it helps me to forgive their children."
–Louis Johannot

Alone

Susan sat alone in her classroom eating her lunch as she did every day. The only sound was the clicking of the ceiling fan which was the only means of relief on this sticky May day.

Her students loved their innovative and creative teacher. She could turn mundane facts into lessons of real-life intrigue. She could motivate unwilling children in a single year. And when she was nominated "teacher of the year," no one was surprised. But just like Superman, this super teacher felt very much alone among her colleagues.

Susan was not the only exceptional teacher at her school; she was just the one who gained the most attention. Attention from the local media. Attention from supervisors and from students' parents.

Then why does she dine alone each day? Peer jealousy. It infects even the best of schools. It can destroy healthy relationships and kill morale.

How do you reverse its effects? One way is by reaching outside yourself to others, giving them a priority in your mind. Another way is to include others in your innovations and share the credit.

YOU CAN'T CREATE A SHARED VISION BY BEING A LONE RANGER. REMEMBER TO INCLUDE OTHERS IN YOUR PLANS, AND THEY WILL REMEMBER TO INCLUDE YOU. IF BUILDING YOURSELF UP IS TEARING OTHERS DOWN, THEN IT'S TIME TO RETHINK YOUR PRIORITIES.

A relationship with which I am struggling could improve if I am willing to . . .

"Behind every able man there are always other able men."
–Chinese Proverb

Floor Show

Pamela disliked what she considered to be a teacher's uniform. It was usually a simple dress or more often, in an elementary setting, it was a jumper or denim dress that was decorated with a variety of attention-grabbing paraphernalia such as button covers, I Love Teaching badges, and pins for every holiday and occasion. Pamela wore pants each and every day at her middle school. It was practical and even necessary. It's not that she faulted anyone else for the way they dressed, but a dress would just get in her way.

Sixth graders are a joy to teach. They are still young enough to get excited about learning but old enough to have the skills to produce quality work. Pamela knew it was a challenge to hold their attention at times, but she never ran out of ways to pique their curiosity. This was especially true right before Christmas break when all minds were somewhere else and not on the lesson at hand. Pamela launched one of her most reliable interest-seeking tools.

Amidst the chaos of students settling in after the bell had rung, students stumbled over something on the floor. It was Pamela! She was sitting right in the middle of the room peering into an opaque container, seemingly unaware of their stumblings. Moments later all the students were on the floor beside her, quietly waiting for some explanation.

Pamela continued the lesson while sitting on the floor for the remainder of the class period—her students' attention fixed and firm. It's a good thing she wore pants, huh?

GETTING DOWN TO A STUDENT'S LEVEL SOMETIMES REQUIRES YOU TO ACTUALLY GET DOWN ON THE FLOOR!

Ways I can get down to my students' level are . . .

"When you are dealing with a child, keep your wits about you and sit on the floor."

–Austin O'Malley

The Note

Joyce could never do anything to please Mrs. Raymond. After three years at Charter Middle School, she walked the halls timidly avoiding her principal. Three humiliating classroom observations and conferences with her had made Joyce feel insignificant and insecure.

The next year another principal was transferred to their school, and like before, Joyce avoided contact with her whenever possible.

Then one morning, Mrs. Baker, the new principal, popped into Joyce's room. She took a seat at the back of the class, unnoticed by the students, and stayed for the entire lesson!

Joyce worried. This observation was unannounced, and she was sick at the thought of what was to come.

Later that day, Joyce found a note in her mailbox.

"Thanks for a delightful morning. It always encourages me to see a good teacher in action. Keep up the good work!"

This small act of kindness encouraged Joyce and several other teachers to stay on at the school and continue to perform their best.

A change in principals almost always generates some staff turnover in a school. Those who fell into line with the previous administration are apprehensive about the changes that are sure to come. Yet most times, change is good.

Try to keep an open mind regarding change. Don't let your fears hinder bright possibilities. Remember how you benefit from simple acts of kindness and then bestow those same gifts on your students.

Some ways I can encourage my students with acceptance are . . .

"There is a great man, who makes very many feel small. But the real great man is the man who makes every man feel great."
–G.K. Chesterton

VIP

by Tony Horning

They saw him on the school property, walking around and looking at the ground as if he'd lost something. Later in the day, they saw him picking up trash around the playground. During recess, they saw him pulling weeds from the flower beds in front of the school. He was dressed much nicer than a custodian. He wasn't a teacher. *Who is this man?* the students wondered.

Mrs. Nader's kindergarten class was just beginning to get to know their school, its teachers, and its staff. They'd met Mrs. Ludy, the lunch lady, because she served them in the cafeteria every day. They knew Mr. Foster, the custodian, because he fixed their sink once. And they knew Miss Dansen, the secretary, because they delivered the attendance to her each morning. By the end of the first week, they knew most of the important people.

Then on Friday, the man they saw picking up trash and weeding the garden came into their classroom. He brought their teacher a bouquet of flowers and said, "Kids, you have one of the best teachers in the whole world. I hope you enjoyed your first week of school."

"Who is that man, Mrs. Nader?"

Mrs. Nader chuckled. "That's Mr. Clark, our principal. He cares a lot about our school and wants to keep it looking as nice as possible."

"He sure works hard."

"Yes, he does," she said.

If you think you're a servant, check your reaction the next time you're treated like one.

Some things I can do for my school that would show a servant's heart are . . .

"Servant of All is a greater title than King of Kings."
–F. Crane

Expectations

The challenge of motivating students occupies much of a teacher's time and resources. You have constant thoughts such as, *If I could just get into their hearts, I know I could get through to them.*

You hope they care enough to try and excel. You certainly want them to excel!

It wasn't until graduate school that Anna realized the power of expectations.

Her professor told his students that he expected to see only A's and from them. He spelled out what to do to get a B and what to do to get an A. Assuming they all wanted A's, he went into the greatest detail, outlining specifically how to get one.

Could this work in my classroom? Anna wondered.

To her amazement, the first time she tried this a quarter of her students expressed their desire to work toward an A. Three-quarters chose to work for a B.

By the end of the year, more than 80 percent of her students actually achieved higher grades than they did the period before!

This exercise in expectations was triumphant—for both the students and the teacher.

Keep your expectations for your students high. Mix those expectations with large doses of encouragement and you will discover a class full of achievers!

NEVER UNDERESTIMATE THE POWER OF EXPECTATION.

The way I can use the power of expectation in my class is . . .

"Shoot for the moon. Even if you miss it you will land among the stars."

–Les (Lester Louis) Brown

Together Forever

Shelly was frantic. Two of her sixth graders were still failing, even after numerous attempts on her part to bring them up to speed. Only six weeks remained until their fate would be determined.

She had tried after-school tutoring, peer tutoring, and adjusting her teaching methods. These two students were completely different economically, ethnically, intellectually, and personally. They had only one thing in common—their parents' apparent lack of involvement in their education.

Finally Shelly met with each boy, hoping to gain some insight into his learning styles and motivation.

All Shelly got out of Jason, the first student, was, "I don't know." Discouraged and still no closer to a solution, she met with the second student, Michael.

"Is Jason going to fail? Will he have to go to summer school? If I fail, can we go to the same summer school?" The student flung question after question at Shelly. Then it hit her!

"Michael, are you failing on purpose so you can stay with Jason?"

Michael hesitated but then said, "Someone has to. He's my friend, and now that his dad is out of work, he feels safe only with me."

It explained everything.

"Okay Michael, let's work on this together. Instead of both of you failing together, how about if you succeed together?"

Dig a little deeper and, if you still come up empty, go back and dig deeper still.

A student situation I may need to reconsider and dig deeper to understand is . . .

"All our children deserve teachers who believe they can learn and who will not be satisfied until they do."
–Joe Nathan

Just Julie

Julie loved teaching preschool, and the fact that her students were special needs children only made her job more enjoyable. She felt like she was an intimate part of their lives.

Upon meeting parents, she always insisted that they call her by her first name. At only twenty-two, she hated being called Miss Julie—or even worse, Miss Haler. Even her students called her by her first name. She wanted them to think of her as their trusted friend, not just their teacher.

As the year progressed, Julie grew more and more weary of the daily lessons on living. Many of her students were not potty trained, even at four. But it really wasn't the fact that she had to change diapers that bothered her. It was their unresponsiveness to her attempts to control their outbursts that puzzled Julie and left her exhausted. Sometimes parents volunteered in her class, and on those days the children seemed easier to train.

On one particularly patience-trying day, Julie excused herself to go to her office and regain her composure. What was she doing wrong? Even though she had a parent volunteer, not one student was obeying her. Just as she reentered the classroom, she overheard a parent reprimanding her own daughter, who had been unusually tempestuous that day.

"Alexandra, I expect you to listen to your teacher!" Mom said sternly.

"Why Mom? It's just Julie," Alexandra said, leaving Julie in shock—yet with her answer.

FINDING IT DIFFICULT TO MAINTAIN CONTROL?
CHECK TO MAKE SURE YOU'RE STILL THE TEACHER.

How do you maintain a close relationship with your students and still remain in control?

"What a teacher thinks she teaches often has little to do with what students learn."
—Susan Ohanian

Why?

"Learn Critical Thinking Skills in 100 Easy Lessons?" Sammie asked. "What kind of book is this?"

"The one from our Critical Thinking Skills workshop, remember?" Judy said with a yawn.

"Even if they are easy lessons, I don't have time to teach one hundred of them, do you?" Sammie knew she sounded negative, but she was tired of being told what to teach and how.

"Did anyone think critically about including this in our daily lessons?"

"Doubt it," Judy said.

"I have an idea. Let's figure out a way to encourage critical thinking without using this book," Sammie suggested.

"You don't need to tell me," Judy explained. "I've always taught my students to think about why they do what they do, and how to use what they learn in their everyday lives. It's a matter of attitude."

Sammie realized that Judy didn't need this textbook. But at the same time, she knew that she did. "How can I have that attitude?" Sammie questioned.

Judy could see that Sammie was serious now. Concern was written all over her face. "You already do, just by asking the question 'why.' The key is to encourage your students to do the same."

TO THINK CRITICALLY IS NOT BEING CRITICAL—
IT'S BEING SMART.

A "why" in my life that I am pondering is . . .

"The function of education is to teach one to think intensively and to think critically. Intelligence plus character—that is the goal of true education."
—Martin Luther King Jr.

What He Left Behind

Freshman English was a huge class, and seventeen-year-old Jerry Jenkins cringed at the prospect of it. Already he knew that many professors expected students to figure it out for themselves, and their fifty-minute classes were drudgery to get through. But Dr. Glenn Arnold was different.

From day one Jerry noticed an enthusiasm and commitment in this professor. The man actually enjoyed what he taught and showed more than just polite tolerance to his students. Dr. Arnold showed personal interest in all of them. He was completely prepared for each class and made what is usually just a required subject the highlight of Jerry's college experience. The class was a living testimony to his professor's commitment. And it was catching!

Years later, when Jerry's first book was published, he dedicated it to Dr. Arnold, a professor whose influence reached into classes Jerry now taught. He found out all those years later the secret to Dr. Arnold's success.

"My wife prayed for me every moment I taught," Arnold shared.

The circle of commitment was now complete. Mrs. Arnold was committed to her husband. Dr. Arnold was committed to his call. And his student Jerry Jenkins, through his commitment to the truth, was able to give back to his professor the good things he had reaped as a result of both Dr. and Mrs. Arnold's commitment.

YOUR COMMITMENT DOES NOT GO UNNOTICED. IT WILL RETURN TO YOU SOMEDAY.

If I had someone praying for me every day, I would want them to pray for . . .

"Teachers believe they have a gift for giving: it drives them with the same irrepressible drive that drives others to create a work of art or a market or a building."

—A. Bartlett Giamatti

Involuntary Transfer

Jan's involuntary transfer to an elementary school was difficult. Not only did she prefer middle school, but she felt inadequate to teach at the elementary level. Just because she was certified in that area didn't mean she wanted to teach it.

Teaching in a self-contained classroom all day was quite an adjustment for Jan. Her first method of coping was to keep to herself and observe.

After the first grading period, she realized there was more to being an elementary teacher than wearing theme jewelry and giving out stickers. Her demands on her students were too high and she knew it. She could tell that from the looks on their faces when she assigned research reports. She could also tell it from their parents as note after note came in with complaints. She just didn't know what to do about it all.

During her third-grade team meeting, Jan sat and listened to Kathy, a first-year teacher. Kathy's students loved her. Her room was bursting with energy and creativity. Even her discipline problems were minimal.

How does she do that? Jan wondered. Then, in a moment of utter humility, she said aloud, "How do you do that?"

That was the beginning of a beautiful friendship and a successful school year!

Don't be afraid to ask questions of team members you admire or to share tips with someone new.

FIND SOMEONE WHO IS ALREADY DOING WELL WHAT YOU WANT TO BE DOING WELL, AND THEN ASK THEM HOW THEY DO IT.

Some questions I have in an area I feel weak in are . . .

"Take the attitude of a student. Never be too big to ask questions. Never know too much to learn something new."
–Og Mandino

On My Honor

Steve cringed when he read the duty roster. In addition to his regular hall duty between classes, he also had to monitor the entire seventh-grade hallway during his free period.

"Just great!" Steve murmured. He knew that most teachers didn't bother to stand outside their doors between classes. He also knew that he was on his own if there was trouble. It seemed it would take a fire in the building to get some teachers away from their desks.

Steve watched the corridor for signs of unrest, but only minor infractions cropped up.

"Walk!"

"Get to class!"

"Ladies, this is not a beauty parlor."

Everyday reprimands.

Then suddenly, the hallway exploded with voices. Steve made his way quickly toward the far end of it. There were eight classrooms in close proximity, but each door was closed to the turmoil in the hallway.

A girl was lying on the hard tile floor, her body shaking violently. Her seizure frightened some and amused others, yet no one moved to help. Steve threw open the nearest door and slammed the call button. A teacher still at her desk looked bewildered. "Student down! Get help now!" Steve barked.

YOUR SENSE OF DUTY TO YOUR STUDENTS DOESN'T END INSIDE THE WALLS OF YOUR CLASSROOM. DUTY IS WHERE DUTY CALLS.

I feel God calling me to a sense of duty to my students outside the classroom when . . .

"If there is anything that we wish to change in the child, we should first examine it and see whether it is not something that could better be changed in ourselves."

–Carl Jung

Love Your Job

Since the first grade, Ellen knew she wanted to be a teacher. She could remember setting her bedroom up like a classroom and making her four siblings be the students.

Her first-grade teacher, Mrs. Robinson, loved her students. They in turn loved her and loved to learn. Ellen wanted to instill that same love in others, so she became a teacher.

Most people agree that teachers don't get paid enough. You have to be in it for more than money. You have to love to teach.

Ellen always felt on fire when she was teaching. When a lesson clicked, it was an exhilarating feeling.

Once in a while she'd give students a chance to teach the class when they knew the material well enough to make a presentation. Those who volunteered did so out of desire, not because of outside pressure. She could see future teachers among her students. She could see their love for learning.

So when the union couldn't negotiate a raise or the budget was cut again and her materials were meager, she was still happy.

Ellen was doing what she loved, and she did it well.

REMEMBER TO TEACH FROM YOUR HEART,
NOT FROM DUTY. WHEN YOU DO WHAT YOU LOVE,
YOU WILL DO IT WELL,
NO MATTER THE CIRCUMSTANCES.

The things I love about teaching that keep me happy no matter the circumstances are . . .

"Work is love made visible."
–Kahlil Gibran

The Power of Love

Claire walked through the crowded hallway as if in a fog. She was only remotely aware of her son's tiny hand in hers as they approached his kindergarten classroom. The sights, the smells, and the sounds transported Claire back all those years ago to the day her own mother walked her to kindergarten. Where had the years gone? Everyone said that children grow up so fast. And everyone was right. Here was her little man all ready for school. It was a milestone, a day of ceremony and celebration.

Miss Sauri recognized the look on this mother's face even before she was inside the room. This was a face of a good mother, one whose love for her child showed from top to bottom. The trust between mother and son was communicated in a glance. Mom hung up his backpack and then knelt to give him instructions. Her son nodded in complete understanding and then turned to look at Miss Sauri with those same trusting eyes. Mom has done a good job, Miss Sauri thought.

Then Claire led her son to his teacher. Taking his hand and placing it in hers, she said, "He's all yours."

"No," Miss Sauri said. "He's yours. He's just on loan to me for now."

NEVER UNDERESTIMATE THE POWER OF A MOTHER'S LOVE. IT'S THAT LOVE THAT WILL HOPEFULLY BE TRANSFERRED TO YOU.

A mother's love for her child was a support to me as a teacher one time when . . .

"There is no influence so powerful as that of the mother, but next in rank of efficacy is that of the schoolmaster."

–Sarah Josepha Hale

Problem Solvers

Nancy's sixth-grade class buzzed with excitement as they worked on their semester project: Find a problem within the school and generate solutions and a plan of action to solve it. Nancy had taken a creative problem-solving class during her master's studies and was anxious to try out the technique with her own students. But the first few days of the process turned into one gripe session after another.

"We don't feel like we belong."

"We don't have a student council."

"The eighth graders pick on us in the halls."

On and on it went, one complaint after another. It was a mess, and Nancy needed to help her students focus on what the real problem was before they could ever consider trying to solve it.

"Let's try to formulate a problem this way: In what way(s) might we ____________?" The students then listed all the problems they could think of in this way. After looking at the problems stated on the board, Nancy asked her students if they could think of one problem that narrowed down the mess. They did.

"In what way(s) might we build a sense of community in our school?" Reverent silence followed the realization that they had actually adequately stated the real problem. That was the hard part. Now brainstorming solutions wouldn't be so hard. They were focused and ready for action.

THE FIRST STEP TO SOLVING A PROBLEM IS TO BE ABLE TO STATE IT IN A CONCISE WAY.

Some problems in my school which may be related to each other by a root problem are . . .

"A problem adequately stated is a problem well on its way to being solved."
–R. Buckminster Fuller

Words

Deborah was easily intimidated by the parents of her students, especially those who were the most vocal. Fearing the way a principal might view her, she avoided a documented parental complaint in her records at all costs. Deborah followed the path of least resistance and ignored minor student disturbances.

Her conferences were always a mere formality. If a problem was avoidable, she'd avoid it. One specific situation, however, changed her perspective.

A colleague's child was in Deborah's advanced math class. Never expecting this to be a problem, Deborah was quite surprised that the student was not performing to the class standard. In fact, he was failing. Upon checking his records, she found that he actually belonged in a regular math class, not the advanced class.

She met with the mother and fellow teacher about the situation, only to discover that the mother had manipulated the situation and purposefully had him placed in that class.

After going 'round and 'round for an hour about all the help the student needed, Deborah decided to cut to the chase. "What I mean to say is that Steven really belongs in a regular math class."

As expected, her comment didn't go over well, but the information was reluctantly received. They came to terms and moved him to the correct class, and as Deborah had expected, he excelled.

FOLLOWING PROFESSIONAL ETHICS SOMETIMES TAKES COURAGE. NEVER COMPROMISE THE TRUTH OUT OF FEAR OF THE CONSEQUENCES.

A fear I have been struggling with is . . . I can make a change by . . .

"Try to say the very thing you really mean, the whole of it, nothing more or less or other than what you really mean. That is the whole art and joy of words."

–C.S. Lewis

He Said, She Said

"My dad says I don't have to listen to you!"

"You can't make me!"

"You want me to do what?"

Day after day, Sandy's ears stung with the words of her seventh graders. She was beginning to wonder what went on in the homes of these students. No wonder kids didn't respect their teachers. In the first place, it surely sounded as if their parents didn't have any respect for teachers. One child in particular, David, shot remarks at Sandy almost daily. A conference was set with his dad for the next day. Sandy cringed at the thought of what she'd hear from this man as well.

A sullen Mr. Rankin slipped quietly into the seat of a student's desk. Sandy had positioned it so that she could look down at him from her own desk during the conference. Both began the discussion with hesitancy.

"Mr. Rankin, your son is very bright. So much so that it surprises me you've told him he doesn't have to do anything he doesn't want to do," Sandy said.

"That's not how I heard it," Mr. Rankin said. "David says you refuse to help him when he doesn't understand his work."

"Obviously someone important is missing from this conference," Sandy laughed.

"I can take care of that," Mr. Rankin said, opening the classroom door. "Won't you join us, David?"

Make sure all parties who are involved attend a conference.

Some problems I am seeing that may be due to incomplete communication are . . .

"If you promise not to believe everything your child says happens at this school, I'll promise not to believe everything he says happens at home."
—Anonymous

In the Spotlight

Candice was a teacher who wanted to be an integral part of her new school. She had experience in working on yearbooks, chorus, and writing. So becoming involved with these clubs would be natural for her.

Weeks after the school year began, a teacher left unexpectedly. Not only did she leave a hole in the language department, but now they needed a new drama club sponsor.

The principal approached Candice and offered her the job, since she knew Candice was anxious to become involved. But Candice had had no experience with drama. She was reluctant to take on such a big job.

Her principal encouraged her to try. She told Candice she could always quit if she wanted to, so Candice agreed.

What she found out was that she loved drama! She was good at directing, and her organizational skills and attention to detail made that year's production one of the most professional the school had ever done.

When the students presented her with a dozen roses on opening night, Candice couldn't believe she was standing on stage being applauded for efforts she never knew she was capable of.

When you find yourself in the spotlight, even if you were pushed there, you may find that you like it and actually deserve to be there.

SOME OF THE BEST DISCOVERIES ARE MADE WHEN WE SIMPLY TRY.

Something that I have been timid about trying is . . .

"Until you try, you don't know what you can't do."

–Henry James

A Time to Plan

by Helen Peterson

"Congratulations on your retirement," Trevor, a first-year teacher, told Jim. "We are at opposite ends of this career, aren't we?"

"Not entirely. Retirement sneaks up on you very quickly. Have you begun to plan for your retirement yet?"

That question seemed odd to ask such a young teacher, so Trevor asked him to elaborate.

"There's so much to consider, it's a shame to wait until the last few years," Jim began. "First, if you decide to teach in another town or district in state, please consider keeping your retirement plan intact. It's so expensive to buy those years back. And have you considered a savings plan yet?"

"Yes, I started one just this year," Trevor answered proudly.

"Good for you!" Jim told him sincerely. "Another important consideration, then, is this: keep interested in life. Don't let your career engulf all your time. Take time to develop deep relationships and explore hobbies and fitness sports. I read somewhere that you carry into retirement the interests you have nurtured all your life. So, you see, you've got to get busy right now. Go for it! By the way, have you signed my book, *Oh, the Places You'll Go!*, by Dr. Seuss?"

As Trevor munched on a piece of Jim's retirement cake, he vowed to follow this sage advice.

REMEMBER, IT'S NEVER TOO EARLY TO PREPARE TO RETIRE. MAKE LESSON PLANS FOR YOUR STUDENTS AND LIFE PLANS FOR YOURSELF.

Some interests and friendships I need to cultivate now are . . .

"Light tomorrow with today!"
–Elizabeth Barrett Browning

Success

Teacher in-service is a necessary evil.

With so many changes being implemented, it's difficult to stay up on what is expected. Training is demanded and budgets are crunched in order to meet the needs.

Workshops take up almost every free moment. When you sit in an auditorium full of hundreds of teachers (many of whom would rather be somewhere else) and learn about a promising new strategy, have you ever noticed that only a few actually carry out the recommendations?

That's because it depends on whether or not a teacher is returning to a school that values innovation and embraces change. It depends on whether there is an administrator who frees up teacher time so they can employ new approaches. It depends on the needs of the teacher.

How similar is this phenomenon to what happens in your classroom every day? You teach a new concept and only a small percentage latch onto it right away.

The future success of your students will depend on whether or not you have created an environment that welcomes questions. It depends on whether you give them the time they need to master topics. It depends on whether you're meeting the needs of your students.

SET YOUR STUDENTS UP FOR SUCCESS.

I can create an environment conducive to success by . . .

"The rain falls on all the fields, but crops grow only in those that have been tilled and sown."
–Chinese Proverb

Failed Lesson

John planned his study on multicultural appreciation down to the letter. He gave his students free reign when it came to presenting their projects and envisioned all kinds of creative multimedia presentations. With so many interesting projects to choose from—he couldn't wait to see what they would come up with.

Finally the day arrived and John began to call the students up to make their presentations. After five less-than-earth-shattering presentations, he discovered that less than half of the class had completed the assignment. It was obvious that this was not just a typical situation.

Notes from frustrated parents were thrust in his face.

What had gone wrong?

John decided to stop everything and find out why this lesson had become such an obstacle for his students.

He read the notes from the parents again and began to realize that he had overwhelmed his class with abstract guidelines and expectations. The idea was great. But John had to humble himself and admit to both the students and parents that he should have been more definitive in his expectations.

His humble attitude eventually earned him the loyalty of his students.

Allow creativity to define your projects, but be sure to clarify the guidelines for completing them. As a result, your students can exceed your expectations by courageously and creatively stepping out in their assignments.

If a great many of your students fail at some task, leave your pride at the door and look to yourself for solutions.

Describe a time when you had to reevaluate your teaching style.

"Failure is only the opportunity to begin again more intelligently."
–Henry Ford

Defensive End

Denise couldn't believe she was involved in this kind of conversation once again. *Outsiders have no clue as to why schools make the decisions they make,* she thought. Although an insider herself, Denise frequently didn't know why they made the decisions they made. Regardless of that fact, it was time once again to defend the public school system to her friends.

"What I don't understand is why they use a math program that clearly doesn't reach that many children."

"I want to know why there aren't enough textbooks so my daughter can bring one home to do her homework."

The problem was that Denise had no answers for these questions. She knew that districts made decisions that sometimes made no sense to her or to any other teacher. She also knew that she and many others like her had dedicated their lives to public education because they believed they could make a difference in their students' lives.

She answered with confidence, "It's true that there are plenty of problems with the system, but let me tell you why I think the time I give to public education is important." Denise then shared with her friends her passion for teaching and some experiences from her classroom which kept her believing that she was touching lives and that learning was happening, even with the system's imperfections.

THE BEST ASSET OF ANY SCHOOL IS ITS DEDICATED TEACHERS. WHEN PEOPLE COMPLAIN TO YOU ABOUT WHAT YOUR SCHOOL DOESN'T HAVE, GENTLY REMIND THEM OF WHAT, AND WHO, IT DOES HAVE TO OFFER.

Some of the most important assets I believe I offer my school are . . .

"School is the marketplace of possibility, not efficiency."

–Susan Ohanian

Babe Ruth

A few months after his seventh birthday, George (Babe) Ruth was labeled a juvenile delinquent and was sent to the St. Mary's Industrial School for Boys. The years he lived there turned his life around.

At St. Mary's, George had to follow a strict regimen of activities that included religious instruction, academic studies, industrial training, and athletics. George, of course, excelled on the athletic field.

But it was more than athletics that saved George Ruth.

Brother Matthias took the boy under his wing and encouraged him to take advantage of his talents. Matthias was a fair man, and George, who was considered one of the school's biggest troublemakers, respected him. Matthias, who was responsible for putting Ruth on the right track, gave George the love and attention he never received from his own father.

Ruth later said that Brother Matthias was "the greatest man I've ever known."

Is there a Babe Ruth in your classroom? A troublemaker whose talent has yet to be harnessed? You know who he is. He's the one you wish would be absent, but he never is.

MAYBE YOU WILL BE THE TEACHER TO POINT HIM OR HER IN THE RIGHT DIRECTION.

A Babe Ruth in my class is . . . One way I can point them in the right direction is . . .

"The good life, as I conceive it, is a happy life. I do not mean that if you are good you will be happy—I mean that if you are happy you will be good."
—Bertrand Russell

Whom Do You Owe?

Stan was in a state of shock after his annual evaluation. There were too many check marks in the "Needs Improvement" column. Since he was teaching on an annual contract basis, he knew that if things didn't improve, the school was under no obligation to rehire him. Stan waited for the principal to remark on his failings.

The principal knew this had been a difficult year for Stan. The premature death of his wife had left him both numb and overwhelmed with the responsibilities of caring for their three children. What Stan really needed today was support, not ultimatums.

"I know you must feel overwhelmed right now, Stan. I'm personally going to work alongside you and help you in the areas where you've fallen behind. In fact, I'll do much of it myself," the principal said.

Stan was so relieved by his principal's kindness that he returned to class with a new lease on life. As his students filed in, he checked the grade book for missing assignments. "Justin!" he shouted across the room. "Looks like you owe me two assignments. I expect them by the end of the day, or I'll drop you one letter grade."

As the student paled and panic swept his face, Stan remembered his own panic about his evaluation and the grace that had been extended to him. He called Justin to his desk and said, "On second thought, why don't you come by after your last class, and we'll work on those missing assignments together."

In need of grace? Don't forget to extend it to someone else as well.

When in your life did someone extend you grace at a difficult moment? How did it make you feel?

"It is a mystery why adults expect perfection from children. Few grownups can get through a whole day without making a mistake."

–Marcelene Cox

Say It Isn't So!

The caller's question made Junetta sigh. So often when she did these radio shows, parents would call in with questions that made her look like a hero. But this question always made Junetta nervous. She knew her answer could make many parents angry with her. Yet she couldn't avoid the truth. It would be wrong for her to reinforce wrong thinking.

"My son's teacher wants to hold him back in second grade, but I don't agree with her. How can I convince the principal that the teacher is wrong?"

Junetta chose her words carefully but then said them with confidence. "The truth is that principals discourage teachers from recommending retention. It doesn't look good on a school's record if they have retentions. But if this principal is standing behind his teacher's decision, I would take heed. She wouldn't have made this recommendation unless she was sure."

"But his sister did so well at this school. He can, too, if we just move him forward," the caller said, sounding desperate.

"I understand your concern, but I am more concerned about your son's future. Just because his sister did well in this school doesn't mean he will. What works with one does not always work with another. Instead of forcing him into something before he's ready, why don't you give him the gift of time?" Junetta waited through silence for the caller's reply.

"I never looked at it that way. Thank you."

COMMUNICATING THE TRUTH TO SOMEONE WITHOUT ALIENATING THEM IS A DIFFICULT JOB, BUT THE TRUTH WILL PREVAIL.

I have found that the best way to communicate the truth effectively is to . . .

"Nothing fruitful ever comes when plants are forced to flower in the wrong season."
–Bette Bao Lord

Reach for the Stars

Barb was used to having children with special needs in her fourth-grade classroom. She knew how to modify the curriculum to fit her students individually.

Parents were appreciative of her open-mindedness, and their children succeeded in her class.

One year, Barb was faced with a child whose needs she had never encountered before.

Chris had one of the highest IQ's she had ever seen. He scored four years above his grade level on standardized tests. But Chris had become lazy and would only do the bare minimum of work. Even so, his bare minimum was still higher than the rest of his class. He got straight A's, but Barb knew he could do more.

Barb decided to raise the bar for Chris. She defined for him a separate list of expectations. At first Chris balked at the change. His comfort level was threatened. For the first time in his short academic career, Chris wasn't sure he'd get an A. He had to work for it.

After a few weeks of careful monitoring, Chris had regained his passion for learning. He began to crave challenge, and Barb gave it to him. She kept him on his toes, and he kept her on hers.

Never let your students accept the status quo. Push them; let them taste the satisfaction and exhilaration that come from a hunger for knowledge.

Teach your students to reach, and they'll never stay on the ground.

One way to raise the bar for my students is . . .

"Treat people as if they were what they ought to be and you help them to become what they are capable of being."
–Johann Wolfgang von Goethe

Personal Image

This was her first faculty meeting! Amy scanned the room, looking for a familiar face, and found none. She felt more like it was her first day of school. Everyone else settled into their seats as if they owned them. Familiar cliques reunited after a long, restful summer. *Just think,* Amy thought. *We're all here for the same reason. We have the same mission.*

Amy couldn't help but overhear the conversations going on in front of and behind her. She knew everyone must be as excited as she was to welcome the children—their children. Amy was wrong.

"Can you believe it?" someone behind her said. "They moved all my stuff just so they could paint the room! They didn't even have the decency to put it back the way I had left it!"

Then in front of her, "Look at her! She thinks just because she's a dean that she has power over us. It was only a few months ago that she was just a teacher like us."

And then right next to her, "You've got to be kidding! Look at my roster. More than five students in special education. What do they expect me to do? Work miracles?"

Where was the love of teaching? Where was the humility in knowing you would shape young minds? Amy looked in her pocket mirror for the answer. "I hope I never forget why I'm here," she whispered to the image.

WHEN YOU CAN'T REMEMBER WHY YOU'RE WHERE YOU ARE, LOOK IN THE MIRROR AND ASK ONE PERSON WHO STILL REMEMBERS.

Three reasons I am here are . . .

"No one should teach who is not in love with teaching."
—Margaret E. Sangster

Order! Order!

Teaching is one of the few professions that requires an immediate replacement for you if you're absent.

It takes more than written lesson plans in order for a substitute to effectively teach your class in your absence. It also takes organization.

Do you know a teacher whose room is one big pile of papers and books? Whose desk isn't evident to the human eye? Whose supplies spill into crevices and corners and whose files are files in name only?

That teacher puts a substitute in peril when he or she takes over a class.

How can a teacher help a substitute? Leave directions and detailed lesson plans. Let the substitute know where the teacher's manuals are. Where the grade book is. Where the supplies lay hidden.

When substitutes have to rely on students in order to find things, they aren't able to adequately cover the material. They appear helpless and lose control of the classroom. They feel frustrated and may never come back.

Many teachers complain that they are not considered as professionals by the world.

By the world's standards, how professional is your classroom? Remember, your room is a direct reflection on you.

NEED HELP GETTING ORGANIZED?
FIND SOMEONE WHOSE CLASSROOM YOU ADMIRE AND ASK THEM FOR HELP.

I admire the classroom of a colleague because . . . I would like to ask them for help in . . .

"A place for everything, and everything in its place."
–Samuel Smiles

The Gardener

Susan learned long ago that not every child will achieve on grade level. Teaching severely learning-disabled middle-schoolers gave her a chance to take students far, just not as far as the state was hoping for. By the time students had gotten to her, their fourth-grade reading level was probably as high as they were going to go. Instead of looking to see how well they scored on the standardized tests, Susan concentrated on individual skills and learning strategies. She knew they could improve, but she wasn't going to disappoint herself and her students by expecting more than they could give.

"Aren't you being a defeatist?" her intern asked.

"Not at all," Susan said. "I've just learned that it doesn't matter how lovingly you plant a seed, nor does it matter how rich the soil is or how well it is watered and fed; some grow only as tall as we imagined they would."

"Doesn't that disappoint you?"

"It used to. But now I've learned to see the beauty of each one, no matter how tall it grows or how glorious it blossoms," Susan said. She knew her intern didn't understand this flowery talk. But she knew that those who don't achieve as we hope are not weeds to be plucked out so the garden looks perfect. If you've ever tried to transplant a weed, you know that it doesn't survive. It grows stronger if allowed to stay right where it is.

SET YOUR STUDENTS UP FOR SUCCESS BY SETTING REALISTIC EXPECTATIONS FOR THEM.

How does my attitude compare to the one portrayed?

"You take people as far as they will go, not as far as you would like them to go."
–Jeannette Rankin

Laugh

Justin was the class clown. There wasn't a day that went by that he didn't interrupt some lesson with his quick wit. He saw "funny" written all over everything.

You have to be careful with the class clown; however, he or she can easily take over your class, and Mr. Watkins had decided early on that this would never happen in his room.

But it became a challenge to Justin to make Mr. Watkins laugh. Justin realized that it had to be carefully planned. He also realized that it could happen more easily if he completed all his work so Mr. Watkins wouldn't have anything to complain about.

What Justin didn't know was that Mr. Watkins was struggling every day not to laugh. He didn't want to give Justin the satisfaction.

But Justin was hilarious! The more Mr. Watkins avoided eye contact, the more Justin attracted attention to himself. It was becoming a stressful situation for Mr. Watkins. He began getting tension headaches and would end the day in a grumpy mood.

Then one day it happened. Mr. Watkins let go and laughed out loud!

The class was shocked; the clown was jubilant! The teacher was relieved.

Headaches gone, Mr. Watkins realized that laughter really was the best medicine. He decided to take a dose each day.

If handled well, laughter can be used to your advantage. Let students see you laugh, and you let them see your heart.

Things that make me laugh are . . .

"A good laugh is sunshine in a house."
–Thackeray

Jimmy

Jimmy challenged his teacher day after day.

The lesson was always interrupted to deal with some outburst or rule infraction. Mrs. Jenkins tried strict adherence to her discipline plan. She tried ignoring his behavior. She even tried bribing Jimmy. All these solutions were short-lived. They were Band-Aids when only holistic care would do.

As all teachers do, Mrs. Jenkins knew her students quite well. She knew Jimmy's likes and dislikes, strengths and weaknesses, gifts and talents. And she decided to try a combination approach that would address the whole child and not just his behavior.

Since Jimmy was artistic, Mrs. Jenkins gave him the responsibility of making posters. Since he worked better alone than in a group, she assigned him specific tasks at group times. And since he like attention, she called on him for answers even before he could raise his hand.

In time, Jimmy's outbursts decreased. His productivity increased. Mrs. Jenkins had found a better way for Jimmy and for herself.

Try to always remember, your students are more than a set of behaviors. They are people who have needs, desires, and preferences. When problems arise, look past the situation and into the child.

Know your students well enough to identify what they need. Then give it to them.

Choose not to label your students by their behaviors. Help them evolve into something better than they thought they could be.

Recall a time when you were able to use a troublesome student's strengths to empower him to be successful.

Education is helping the child realize his potentialities."

–Erich Fromm

The Right Answer

"What would it be like if," Miss Chandler asked her wide-eyed sixth graders, "we suddenly had to live without electricity?"

Silence. No hands rising. Questioning looks.

"Come on," she coaxed. "Just yell out ideas." Again, silence.

"Okay, I'll start you off." Miss Chandler proceeded to list three things they would have to do if they didn't have electricity anymore. Slowly but surely the students sat up a little taller, and the answers started coming.

Afraid that they didn't have the right answer, her students were reluctant to participate in the creative process.

Schools have taught students that the right answer is the one that matters most. So what you see on students' faces when you ask thought-provoking questions is frequently fear!

How can you make your classroom a safe place to dream? To question?

It's more than creative bulletin boards and playing classical music in the background. It's your attitude.

If you believe that there is value in the process, then you must communicate that to your students. They have to know they can give a wrong answer in order to find the right one. And they need to know that sometimes there is more than one right answer!

Most importantly, they need to know that there will be times in life when no answers are available, but seeking answers is always okay.

Is your classroom a safe place to dream?

What dreams has God given me? What will it take for me to make my classroom a safe place for my students to develop their own dreams?

"Imagination is more important than knowledge."
–Albert Einstein

Follow Those Tracks

Jim Spade watched painfully as one of his students stood facing the blackboard for more than five minutes without even making a scribble on it. Day after day, he wondered what she was even doing in his class. She was obviously not up to algebra at the eighth-grade level. Finally, exasperated, Jim said, "Sit down, Miss Downy. Let's give someone else a chance." Jim knew his frustration with this student showed even more than a little. Yet she was in his class, and there was nothing he could do about it. He decided he would not hold back the rest of the students, who clearly belonged there, for this one inept student.

Carolyn Kane read Jim's remarks in the file of this misplaced student. Her heart broke. Where had the mistake been made? She looked at her test scores from last year and found that the student had tested out easily for the advanced math, yet she was failing Jim's class. And now she was absent at least once a week. It was time for a conference, but not with the parents.

Jim's tightly folded arms told Carolyn all she needed to know. Jim felt no obligation to this student. Her failure was a blemish to him, something better ignored than dealt with. Yet it seemed too late in the year to move the student to the regular math class.

Two afternoons a week Carolyn tutored this student. It was not in her job description. It wasn't her problem. But it was necessary for the girl's self-esteem.

BEING WILLING TO GIVE A LITTLE EXTRA TO HELP MEET A STUDENT'S NEED IS WHAT MAKES A GOOD TEACHER GREAT.

Ways that I might need to shift my attitude toward a student in need are . . .

"Woe to him who teaches men faster than they can learn."
—Will Durant

Raise the Bar

Chuck had taught above-average sections of middle-school math for fifteen years. He knew what it took for students to be successful in his classroom and was proud of the job he'd done all those years. Then on the last day of school, the secretary asked him to turn in his teacher's manuals because he would be teaching the below-average sections the next term.

Chuck laughed aloud as he frantically tried to decide whether or not Mrs. Johnson was joking. Something was terribly wrong. His students had all done quite well. Then why had he been demoted? At least that's how he perceived it.

Chuck reluctantly handed his manuals to Mrs. Johnson and turned to leave. His principal caught him by the elbow. "Chuck, I'm glad you're up for the challenge. These kids need you. I want only the best for them."

Chuck wasn't sure whether to thank Mr. Cohen or turn in his resignation. Next year would be far from easy. He couldn't depend on his tried-and-true methods. He'd have to work harder than ever before to reach these kids. Then he realized that that was the source of his resistance. He also realized the opportunity this change could give him.

"Thanks for the opportunity, Mr. Cohen. It was time to shake things up a bit. Don't want to get lazy!" Chuck grabbed his new manuals and began to wonder what he could do to create success in his class next year.

WHEN TEACHING BECOMES TOO EASY, IT'S TIME TO RAISE THE BAR. IF YOU'RE NOT CHALLENGED, YOU DON'T LEARN.

What might raising the bar look like in my own life?

"Teachers who set and communicate high expectations to all their students obtain greater academic performance from those students than teachers who set low expectations."

–Research Finding, U.S. Department of Education

Friends

Cindy and Sharon were expecting babies at the same time this school year. Because they were friends, it made the experience all the more special.

Then one day Sharon didn't come to work. She had miscarried over the weekend. Cindy's sadness for her friend turned into apprehension as she wondered what to say once Sharon returned. She knew she'd be a constant reminder to Sharon of her loss.

When Sharon did return, she walked like a ghost through the school's hallways. No one spoke to her, let alone acknowledged her loss. They didn't know what to say, so they said nothing. Even Cindy found herself avoiding her friend. She knew Sharon was hurting; she simply didn't know what to do about it.

Two weeks later during her free period, Cindy happened upon Sharon in the teachers' lounge. Sharon was supposed to be in class, yet she was here, crying. Cindy instinctively comforted her friend, but then realized Sharon's class was unsupervised.

Sharon was paralyzed with grief and couldn't function. Assuring Sharon that everything would be all right, Cindy ran to the classroom just after the late bell rang.

Cindy took care of Sharon's class that period. It was all she could think to do, yet it was exactly what Sharon needed from her.

USE COMPASSION WHEN DEALING WITH FELLOW TEACHERS, AND ACT SWIFTLY WHEN DUTY CALLS. NEVER USE WORDS WHEN ACTION IS REQUIRED.

Some simple acts of compassion that others have given to me include . . .

"If a friend is in trouble, don't annoy him by asking him if there's anything you can do. Think of something appropriate, and do it."

–E.W. Howe

About the Author

A veteran educator and curriculum designer, Vicki Caruana loves to encourage teachers! She is frequently a featured speaker at conferences for educators, home-schoolers, and parents. Presently she spends most of her time writing for a wide variety of publications, including *Our Children, Focus on the Family,* and *Christian Parenting Today.*

She credits her inspiration to her first-grade teacher, Mrs. Robinson, at Mount Vernon Elementary School, who influenced her decision at age six to become a teacher, and to her family with whom she now lives in Colorado Springs, Colorado.

For additional information on seminars, consulting services, scheduling speaking engagements, or to write to the author, please address your correspondence to: vcaruana@aol.com

Additional copies of this title and other titles from Honor Books are available from your local bookstore.

Apples and Chalkdust™

Apples and Chalkdust™ #2

The Complete Apples and Chalkdust™

Apples and Chalkdust™ Notes

Apples and Chalkdust™ portable

If you have enjoyed this book, or if it has impacted your life, we would like to hear from you.

Please contact us at:

Honor Books,
An Imprint of Cook Communications Ministries
4050 Lee Vance View
Colorado Springs, CO 80918

Or through our website:
www.cookministries.org